Founded in 1964 by John W...
Voices: Journal of the Ameri...

Editor:
 Kristin Staroba, MSW | *kristin.staroba@gmail.com*
 1201 Connecticut Ave., NW, Ste. 710
 Washington DC 20036
Graphic Designer:
 Mary de Wit
Business Manager:
 Lisa Kays
 1800 R Street NW #C-8
 Washington, DC 20009
International Consultant:
 Jacob Megdell, PhD, Canada
Emeriti:
 Penelope L. Norton, PhD, *Immediate Past Editor*
 Doris Jackson, PhD, *Editor Emerita*
 Tom Burns, PhD, *Editor Emeritus*
 Jon Farber, PhD, *Editor Emeritus*
 Monique Savlin, PhD, *Editor Emerita*
 Edward Tick, PhD, *Editor Emeritus*
 E. Mark Stern, PhD, *Editor Emeritus*
 Vin Rosenthal, PhD, *Editor Emeritus*
Associates:
 Hallie S. Lovett, PhD, *Contributing Editor*
 Bob Rosenblatt, PhD, *Intervision Editor*
 Barry Wepman, PhD, *Poetry Editor*
 Ruth Wittersgreen, PhD, *Poetry Editor*

Editorial Re...
 Carla Bauer, LCSW
 Lee Blackwell, PhD
 Brooke Bralove, LCSW-C
 Peggy Brooks, PhD
 Grover Criswell, MDiv
 Susan Diamond, MSW
 Molly Donovan, PhD
 Nicholas Emmanuel, LPC
 Rhona Engels, ACSW
 Stephanie Ezust, PhD
 Pamela Finnerty, PhD
 Natan Harpaz, PhD
 Stephen Howard, MD
 Susan Jacobson, MMH
 Nicholas Kirsch, PhD
 Judy Lazarus, MSW
 Matthew Leary, PhD
 Kay Loveland, PhD
 Laurie Michaels, PhD
 Don Murphy, PhD
 Giuliana Reed, MSW
 Ann Reifman, PhD
 John Rhead, PhD
 Murray Scher, PhD
 Avrum Weiss, PhD
 Sharilyn Wiskup, LPC

VOICES: THE ART AND SCIENCE OF PSYCHOTHERAPY (ISSN 0042-8272) is published by the American Academy of Psychotherapists, 230 Washington Ave Ext, Suite 101 / Albany, NY 12203.

Subscription prices for one year (three issues): $65 for individuals PDF only; $85 for individuals PDF & print copy; $249 for institutions. Orders by mail payable by check: 230 Washington Ave Ext, Suite 101 / Albany, NY 12203. Orders by MasterCard or Visa: call (518) 240-1178 or fax (518) 463-8656. Payments must be made in U.S. dollars through a U.S. bank made payable to *AAP Voices*. Some back volumes may be available from the *Voices* Business Office.

Change of Address: Please inform publisher as soon as a change to your email address is made. Send change of email address to aap@caphill.com.▼

Journal of The American Academy of Psychotherapists

VOICES

THE ART AND SCIENCE OF PSYCHOTHERAPY

Technology is anything that wasn't around when you were born.
—Alan Kay

Journal of the American Academy of Psychotherapists

VOICES
THE ART AND SCIENCE OF PSYCHOTHERAPY

Technology and Psychotherapy Spring 2018: Volume 54, Number 1

Voices: Journal of The American Academy of Psychotherapists i
Table of Contents v

Editorials

Sent from my iPhone	Lisa Kays	1
	Rosemary Moulton	2
	Eileen Dombo	3
Arriving in the 21st Century	Kristin Staroba	4

Articles

The Ten Tech Commandments	Marilyn Schwartz	5
Implements and Weapons: Children, Teens and Digital Media	Penelope Norton	13
Is Social Media the New Imaginary Audience?	Campbell States	21
Text Me When You Get Here: Allowing Technology in the Therapeutic Playroom	Erin McCarthy	23
Technology and Attunement	Eileen Dombo	29
Todd Essig's Conference on Technology and Intimacy	Leyla Mahbod Kenny	34
Sex and Love in the Digital Age	Michael Giordano	41
Life as a Text-Based Therapist	Erika Bugaj	45
A Balancing Act	Anonymous	47
Tech Talk: Cheating Presence or Enhancing It?	Lisa Kays	52
	Damon Blank & Loretta Sparks	53
This Is My Brain on ADHD	Rebecca Wineland	59
Tech Q&A	Lisa Kays, Eileen Dombo & Rosemary Moulton	61
Online Education	Kynai Johnson	65
Fictional Clinical Supervision Notes: Krista Gordon of the TV Show Mr. Robot	Rosemary Moulton	67
Fantasy and Therapy: Psychotherapists on the Not-So-Blank Screen	Jonathan Farber	75
Rearview Mirror—A Fantasy	Tom Burns	79

Review

Screen Relations: The Limits of Computer-Mediated Psychoanalysis and Psychotherapy	Carla R. Bauer	97

Aging and Psychotherapy

AAP Tape Library		83
Tape #3: Carl Rogers, Mr. Vac	Carl R. Rogers	83
Commentary	Ann Reifman	92
	Rhona Engels	94
	Murray Scher	95
Intervision		100
What We Have Here Is a Failure To Communicate	Bob Rosenblatt	100
The Case	Doris Jackson	101
Response 1	Lorraine Hallman	103
Response 2	Arthur S. Weinfeld	104
Response 3	Robert Rosenblatt	105
Poetry		33
The Ego at Sunset	Blake Edwards	33
Wired Shut	Gina Sangster	58
Are you there?	Kathryn Van der Heiden	81
Images		68
Mr. Robot, Episode 3	USA Network	68
Call for Papers		107
WTF?!? Oppression, Freedom, and Self	Deadline August 15, 2018	107
Voices		108
Subscribe to Voices		108
Guidelines for Contributors		109
The American Academy of Psychotherapists		110

On the Front Cover:
Vase or Faces?
2018, Illustration by Mary de Wit
Editorial Illustrations Within: Dreamstime

©2018 by the American Academy of Psychotherapists, Inc.
Published three times per year.
Cover Design: Mary de Wit
Design and Production by
Mary de Wit | inw2Wit®, llc
AAP Web Site:
www.aapweb.com

Editorials

Sent from my iPhone

Lisa Kays

LISA KAYS, LICSW, LCSW-C, is a clinical social worker in private practice in Washington, DC, where she works with individuals, couples and groups. Her professional adventures include writing and training therapists in ethics and social media, as well as integrating improv with therapy. Her improv for therapists classes have been featured on NBC4 and in *The Washington Post*. She lives in Washington, DC, with her husband and almost-three-year-old son, who was asking for a "phon-y" far earlier than she expected.
lisa@lisakays.com

Technology and psychotherapy is a rich topic with many facets. Technology is pervasive in our lives and has affected our most basic human interactions. Even phones in our pockets have dramatically altered the way we navigate roads, dates, and dinner conversations. In thinking about this issue, we looked at it in the broader sense of how technology is impacting relationships, especially the therapeutic relationship. How is it helpful in bringing people closer and fostering connection, and how is it getting in the way? How do we as clinicians experience this connection, and how do our experiences inform our clinical work? Innovations in technology can be life-altering. As the fabric of society changes, we are still there to help others. How do our professional fields keep up? In what ways do we adapt, and in what ways do we remain unwavering? How do we sort through these largely unexpected changes?

Here's what each of the guest editors brings to the table:

Lisa Kays: I conceived this issue out of genuine curiosity. I have been thinking about the intersection of technology and the work of therapists since I was an MSW student at Catholic University of America (CUA), when I was told in most classes that I needed to "get off the Internet" to be a responsible social worker. The rebel part of me of course said no. Other parts were more nuanced. I considered my reluctance to give up Facebook or Twitter in the name of professional integrity and how I might balance my own life with my livelihood. I also considered how the social workers and therapists of younger generations might navigate this, given that most have lived their entire lives leading up to graduate school online. Eileen Dombo helped spark this interest post-graduation when she asked me to speak about a paper I'd written as a student to one of her field instruction classes. When she learned I hadn't been able to publish that paper because of a lack of research and data, she offered to collaborate. We published "Clinical Social Work Practice and Technology: Personal, Practical, Regulatory, and Ethical Considerations for the Twenty-First Century," and then began offering what turned out to be very popular continuing education workshops about the ethics of social workers and social media. It seemed that we weren't the only ones with an interest in and questions about this topic. I later learned that Rosemary Moulton, a fellow CUA grad, was closely reviewing the new social work technical standards and had a strong interest in this topic as well. Eileen and Rosemary seemed like natural guest editors for this issue of *Voices*, and so here we are.

ROSEMARY MOULTON, LICSW, LCSW, is a gender therapist and EMDR therapist in private practice in Arlington, Virginia, and Washington, DC. Her passions include travel and nature, and on the Big 5 she scores high on the openness to experience dimension. She plans to someday expand her practice to include teletherapy to reach underserved populations of LGBTQIA young adults in rural areas. *rmoultonlicsw@gmail.com*

Rosemary Moulton: I too am very curious about the intersection of technology and psychotherapy. Boundaries and personal privacy has been my number-one concern. Working and socializing among people who are marginalized because of gender identity and sexuality has been challenging, because I occupy similar spaces as my clients. Even though the Washington, DC, metropolitan area has approximately 6 million people, I sometimes feel like I have a lot in common with rural therapists because of the relatively small size of the communities I serve. How does one even navigate online dialogues, when some clients are only one degree away as friends of friends on Facebook? The best practices of social media for therapists are ever-changing as technology changes. There are privacy settings, but there can be no reasonable expectation of privacy. One comment on a friend's Facebook post, and I've disclosed how excited I get about the giant panda Bao Bao eating watermelon, or even the intimacy I share with mutual friends. Professional codes of ethics don't spell these things out. Lisa's workshop "Social Media Ethics for Social Workers," offered answers and more questions, as ethics workshops often do. I read through the 80-plus pages of the new technology standards put out by the NASW, ASWB, CSWE, and CSWA, and again was left with more questions than answers. One thing that I do know—I love asking these questions. Editing this issue has given me so much food for thought, and I'm excited to take part in the rich and juicy dialogue about the intersection of technology and psychotherapy.

Eileen Dombo: My interest in this special issue arose from my curiosity about the use of technology in the delivery of mental health services. As an academic and practitioner, I have seen how my students' and clients' use of phones, computers, social media, and the Internet have shifted our interactions. It turns out I wasn't the only one who was curious! This issue allows readers to get a sense of what's happening in the world beyond the couch. We must all ask ourselves how we will engage with technology and how that impacts our practice. As an educator, I also concern myself with how it forms the next generation of therapists. I'm still not on Facebook and don't have a Twitter account, but I am more open to the benefits of technology in our work than ever before.

The interest in topics related to this issue was high, yet prospective authors hesitated. Some asked if they could write anonymously for the issue and expressed nervousness about being judged. In areas of practice in which there is little research, data, or best practices established, we clinicians are often left to make our own ways. Our personal experiences play a big role in how we help others, and perhaps in these under-researched areas we feel most vulnerable and susceptible to criticism by others. This issue then became a way to combat the silos in which many of us are operating when it comes to the influence and use of technology in our practices. This issue, we found, touches on boundaries, self-disclosure, and the therapeutic frame—topics already hotly debated. These are also areas where clinicians are already inserting their own personal preferences, comfort zones, and, ultimately, their selves. Technology, like issues of diversity or religion, is laden with personal bias, strong beliefs, judgments, and assumptions. Putting oneself out there then to discuss it, and particularly its use in clinical practice, is a bold action indeed.

Eileen Dombo

EILEEN DOMBO, PhD, MSW, LICSW is an associate professor, assistant dean, and chair of the MSW program at The Catholic University of America's National Catholic School of Social Service. She teaches practice classes in the program's clinical concentration, and her research interests include clinical models of practice; effective therapeutic intervention techniques for social workers in trauma treatment; and the links between trauma work and vicarious trauma. Dr. Dombo is the former clinical director of the DC Rape Crisis Center and she continues to provide trauma treatment through her private practice and consulting work. Dr. Dombo chairs the Child Protection Board for the Archdiocese of Washington. Based on her work and reputation among her peers, she was named a "Top Therapist" by Washingtonian Magazine.
dombo@cua.edu

Kristin Staroba

Arriving in the 21st Century

KRISTIN STAROBA, MSW, practices in downtown Washington, DC, treating adults in individual, group, and couples psychotherapy. This year is her sixth and last as *Voices* editor, and she will pass the baton to Carla Bauer in 2019. Future issues will continue to feature guest editors; those with a deep interest in a theme are invited to get in touch. *kristin.staroba@gmail.com*

NO MATTER HOW MUCH SOME MAY WISH THEM AWAY, NEW TECHNOLOGIES—DEVICES, APPS, EXPERIENCES—ARE HERE, and more arrive daily, it seems. I FaceTime with distant clients, have a website with an email contact option, and text back and forth about scheduling. I'm not on Facebook and find it disconcerting when LinkedIn suggests I connect with a former client—how does it know I know her? We are inundated with communication vehicles (among other things) that inherently alter how we are with clients. Certainly one may choose to keep one's work tightly boundaried, with technology on the far side, but it behooves us at least to consider what is upon us.

This issue of *Voices* has been masterfully curated by guest editors Lisa Kays, Rosemary Moulton, and Eileen Dombo. Their reach into diverse therapist communities brings a wealth of perspectives and information that will inform, teach, and possibly disturb readers. We hope it provokes some conversation and welcome letters to the editor in response.

Here's a look at what's inside the issue:

Marilyn Schwartz leads off with a comprehensive review of how professional ethics plays out with new technologies. Penelope Norton, Campbell States, and Erin McCarthy look at how new technologies affect children and teens, in and out of our offices. Using the graduate school classroom as a primary source, Kynai Johnson compares in-person to online teaching; Eileen Dombo considers the effect of technology use by therapists in training on learning attunement. Leyla Kenny reports on a workshop by Todd Essig.

Bringing a wider view, Mike Giordano writes candidly about online dating; Erika Bugaj muses on her life as a text-based therapist; and Anonymous shares their process figuring out what boundaries to establish as they bridge identities as performer and therapist.

Lisa Kays shares an hour with Damon Blank and Loretta Sparks in our interview. How technology interfaces with her ADD is shared by Rebecca Wineland. The editorial team provides several answers to common technology questions in a Q&A.

Peppering our theme with dark humor, Rosemary Moulton considers what a TV therapist's supervisor would say to her; Jon Farber waxes nostalgic about TV and movie therapists of yore; and Tom Burns concocts an 18-year-old's fantasy therapist.

In a new occasional series drawn from AAP's remarkable tape library, Carl Rogers works with a hospitalized schizophrenic man; Ann Reifman, Rhona Engels, and Murray Scher comment. Finally, an insightful book review by Carla Bauer; Bob Rosenblatt's deft presentation of an Intervision case by Doris Jackson and responses by Lorrie Hallman, Arthur Weinfeld, and Bob himself; and new poetry by Kathryn van der Heiden, Gina Sangster, and Blake Edwards round out the issue. ▼

The Ten Tech Commandments

Marilyn Schwartz

THE NATIONAL CENTER FOR TELEHEALTH AND TECHNOLOGY (2011) defines "telemental health" as a subset of telehealth that uses electronic technology to provide mental health services from a distance. It includes such terms such as telepsychology, telepsychiatry, telebehavioral health, online counseling, e-health, and e-counseling. In the process of preparing and presenting several professional workshops on emerging technology and clinical practice, I've distilled what I call the Ten Tech Commandments of practicing telemental health.

As with the original Ten Commandments, there is value in identifying the most important ethical and clinical principles to guide us in providing mental health services using existing electronic technology. As technology and, in turn, telemental health (TMH) services are constantly evolving, these principles may provide a road map for best meeting the opportunities and challenges we face in practicing electronically.

Surprisingly, many psychotherapists do not understand that they are, in fact, providing TMH services. I commonly hear, "I don't practice electronically or online; I only email clients to schedule sessions." But TMH includes using any form of electronic communication with clients: telephone, mobile device, email, messaging, chat, video teleconferencing (VTC), social media and Internet self-help websites and blogs. TMH also includes the transmission of any patient health information (PHI) and clinical supervision and consultation provided electronically. Even if a therapist chose to limit electronic communications with clients, the new reality is that the majority of clients, especially younger ones, will expect us to communicate with them electronically.

MARILYN SCHWARTZ, PhD, CGP, has been a psychotherapist in private practice in Washington, DC, for 40 years, providing individual, couples and group therapy and clinical supervision. In 2005, she created the Adult ADHD Center of Washington, a treatment center for adults with ADHD. A long-term member and fellow of AAP, she is chair of the Ethics Committee and has presented ethics workshops locally and nationally on the topic of emerging technology and clinical practice. Marilyn's best advice is: "Splurge on new devices, if you can, to keep up with ever-changing technology and be open to learning new telemental health approaches." DrMarilynSchwartz@gmail.com

1. Thou shalt not harm.
2. Thou shalt be competent.
3. Thou shalt be culturally sensitive.
4. Thou shalt provide informed consent.
5. Thou shalt protect confidentiality.
6. Thou shalt provide standard of care.
7. Thou shalt no cross state lines.
8. Thou shalt not commit insurance fraud.
9. Thou shalt not google or friend clients.
10. Thou shalt not speak falsely online.

#1. Thou shalt not harm.

Professional codes of ethics that govern the practice of psychotherapy in person also apply to services we provide electronically. Central to all professional codes is the principle of *beneficence versus malfeasance,* meaning that our work with clients should benefit and not hurt them. In this regard, our choice to use telemental health approaches should be made on the basis that these services provide help that is equal or superior to that which can be offered in person. A growing body of research (Harris & Youngren, 2011; Benton & Snowden, 2016) shows that clients receiving TMH do as well as clients receiving in-person services. Also, TMH may be a better option for clients who have limited access to services, require specialized treatment, or have disabilities or mental health conditions that prevent in-person treatment.

A good question to ask in providing TMH services is: Whom does it benefit? "The therapist" is never a good answer to this question. As with in-person treatment, a therapist should always have a good clinical rationale for using a specific TMH approach tailored to the presenting problem of the client and document this in the client's record.

Because new technologies create unique challenges (e.g., security issues, software/hardware failures, jurisdictional practice issues, etc.), our major professional organizations have each developed a set of recommendations for TMH practice (American Psychological Association, 2013; National Association of Social Workers, 2005; and National Board for Certified Counselors, 2016). Worthy of note is that APA refers to its recommendations as "guidelines" rather than "standards," which is used by NASW and NBCC. In doing so, APA recognized that as technology and TMH is ever evolving, practice guidelines need to be "aspirational" and not mandatory nor take precedence over a psychologist's clinical judgement.

#2. Thou shalt be competent.

Professional ethics codes direct us to practice within the boundaries of our competence, which means knowledge and skills acquired through education, training, supervision and experience. Unfortunately, a common misunderstanding among therapists is that one's everyday skills using technology or one's clinical skills in providing in-person therapy are transferable and sufficient to provide TMH. Many therapists think, "If I know how to email, text, Skype, or FaceTime with my friends or children, what's the big deal in doing the same with clients?"

According to recently developed technology guidelines established by our professional organizations, competence in practicing TMH is defined in terms of specific technological, clinical, and regulatory knowledge and skills. For example, are your knowledge and skills using the hardware or software required by TMH interventions adequate and up-to-date? Are you familiar with research and best practices in providing TMH? Are you aware of the laws and regulations that govern the practice of TMH in your state or the state where the client resides? Are you aware of the specific TMH standards recently established by your own professional organization?

Fortunately, there are some clear paths to becoming competent in providing TMH services. The Zur Institute (ZurInstitute.com), the Telemental Health Institute (telehealth.org) and the Online Therapy Institute (http:onlinetherapyinstitute.com) were early to the game in providing training in TMH. The Telehealth Certification Institute (telementalhealthtraining.com) is an example of a newcomer, now offering both online training and in-person workshops in major cities offering certification as a TMH provider. As occurred in the coaching field, we might expect rapid growth of TMH training programs (for sure, not all equally good) and stiff competition between them until one emerges as the nationally recognized certification program. So, buyer beware in seeking training and credentialing in TMH.

#3. Thou shalt be culturally sensitive.

There are no geographical barriers to online practice. It allows mental health professionals to provide services globally and to populations diverse in terms of race, ethnicity, language, religion, sexual orientation and being disabled or vulnerable. Practicing online allows therapists to share their special expertise (treating trauma, social anxiety, ADHD, etc.) with clients who might otherwise not have access to the specific treatment approach they need. But, with these opportunities for reaching more clients in need comes the challenge of practicing in a more culturally sensitive way. Therapists need to incorporate specialized knowledge of clients' cultural differences and tailor their approaches to address these differences.

For example, working with a disabled client via video teleconferencing might require special accommodations if the client has physical limitations or requires help using an electronic device. In such cases, the therapist may need to address with the client the following: How can the client's living space be set up to approximate a therapy office or in-person setting? Is there someone in the home who might assist the client with the electronic device used? Can the privacy of the client during VTC sessions be ensured? Recently, I conducted a psychotherapy session using VTC with a long-term client, who was bedridden after a stroke. Before the sessions could take place, we had considerable discussion of privacy because the client occupied the family room in his house and needed assistance from his wife to operate his laptop.

As another example of promoting cultural sensitivity, Standard 2 of the *Standards for Technology and Social Work* (2005) advises social workers to advocate on behalf of clients to gain access to technology so they can receive TMH. Two examples of complying with this standard are: (1) acquiring knowledge of community resources such as public libraries or senior centers that might provide clients access to technology; and (2) acquiring knowledge of recently developed TMH mobile phone software applications (apps) to use with clients whose only access to technology may be their smartphones.

#4. Thou shalt provide informed consent.

Common to all codes of ethics is the standard that we obtain informed consent from our clients. In using TMH, it is important to obtain consent that addresses the unique features and concerns related to TMH. For example, in addition to describing the TMH approach used and its cost, one should describe the benefits, limitations, and risks of using TMH. One should be clear about the difficulty of maintaining confidentiality of electronically transmitted communications and specify steps taken to safely store, access, and protect client's information.

Informed consent should specify an emergency backup plan, which would include emergency numbers for the client and emergency resources in the client's geographic area. In addition, it is important to specify procedures for technical interruptions and failures; e.g., dropped calls, audio or picture quality problems, etc. Therapists should also be clear on the laws and regulations that apply to confidentiality in their own and the client's jurisdiction; e.g., duty to warn and duty to report.

Statistics show that an ever-increasing proportion of the population is using electronic communications and is on social media. Given this new reality, it is recommended that a social media policy be included as part of informed consent. Dr. Keely Kolmes offers an excellent model of a social media policy that spells out how she will interact with clients online. It can be retrieved at: drkkolmes.com/social-media-policy/. A social media policy not only helps to set the therapeutic frame, but protects against breaches of confidentiality and, as discussed below, the risk of engaging in dual relationships through "friending" or messaging on social networking sites.

#5. Thou shalt protect confidentiality.

Using technology to provide TMH services creates new challenges for therapists in terms of the ethical imperative to protect the confidentiality and privacy of clients. Most professional guidelines ask that we take reasonable steps to protect confidentiality by putting security measures in place to safeguard client health information; e.g., passwords, encryption, firewalls, and back-ups on our computers, smartphones, etc. It is our duty to warn clients of the limits to confidentiality whether due to possible recording or tracking of TMH sessions, mandatory reporting, or the potential for recordings to be subpoenaed.

Our professional organizations have spoken from on high: "Thou shalt not use Skype or FaceTime as a videoconferencing platform for online counseling sessions." It's true that many clients and therapists prefer Skype and FaceTime because they're familiar, easy to use, and incur no extra costs. But these platforms weren't meant to provide security nor are they compliant with the Health Insurance Portability and Accountability Act (HIPAA). For example, Skype uses encryption but holds the encryption key. Neither FaceTime nor Skype are able to provide a business agreement, required under HIPAA, because they don't conduct audits or have a protocol for notification of a security breach. Whether or not you are a covered entity under HIPAA, you are advised to comply with HIPAA regulations as our professional organizations have adopted them as practice standards.

Asking a client to sign a disclaimer about limits to confidentiality using Skype or FaceTime doesn't protect you because the therapist, not the client, is held responsible for protecting confidentiality. A better option is to research and purchase one of the many cost-effective plans for a HIPAA-compliant videoconferencing platform. The Telebehavioral Health Institute (www.telehealth.org) offers webinars as well as recommendations for selecting HIPAA-compliant videoconferencing platforms.

#6. Thou shalt provide standard of care.

The shift from providing in-person treatment to TMH services creates different benchmarks for standard of care. For example, as earlier mentioned, it is important to document in the client's record the clinical rationale for why TMH and the specific approach used (online counseling, chat, text, email, etc.) is better or equal to in-person treatment. Do its benefits (e.g., access to care, client's special needs) outweigh its unique risks (e.g., privacy/security breaches, technical issues)? Is the specific TMH approach used supported by research?

A critical question to ask is whether your client is appropriate for distance or online therapy. It is highly recommended that you provide a formal intake, preferably in person, to assess whether TMH services are appropriate, efficacious and safe for a specific client and re-evaluate during treatment. Generally, bad candidates are felt to be clients with an Axis II diagnosis (narcissistic, borderline, dissociative identity disorder, etc.); who have a history of psychosis or suicidal, violent, or abusive tendencies; and clients who are active alcohol or drug abusers.

Standard of care in providing TMH services also involves additional requirements for record-keeping. As mentioned above, the client's record should include a clinical rationale for using TMH, a plan for handling any technological problems, and an emergency plan, including emergency telephone numbers and emergency resources where the client resides. Also, many therapists are unaware that any electronic communications between them and clients (emails, texts, messages, etc.) are required to be part of the client's record. From a risk management perspective, imagine how you would feel about your emails or texts to a client being read out loud, out of context, in a sarcastic manner by opposing counsel in a court of law, or offered as the basis for a licensing board complaint against you.

#7. Thou shalt not cross state lines.

The number-one legal issue involved in providing TMH services is practicing across state lines or what is referred to as interjurisdictional practice. Most states require you to be licensed in the state where the client contact occurs as well as the state where you practice. An exception to this is if you are a mental health professional employed by the military or a federal agency. If you aren't licensed where your client is, you may be committing a criminal offense and nullifying your malpractice insurance coverage. It is, therefore, critical to authenticate the identity of your client and the state where he/she resides.

One option to address interjurisdictional practice issues is to get a temporary license in the state where the client resides. But, as with applying for a permanent license, this could be a tedious and time-consuming process. For psychologists, the Association of State and Provincial Psychology Boards has created two credentials for practicing across state lines, and five states have recently approved it. The expectation is that approval will follow from other states and this model or similar will be adopted by other mental health professions.

8. Thou shalt not commit insurance fraud.

It goes without saying that we are always required to bill clients accurately for the services we provide. If we are working with a client online rather than in-person, we are required to indicate that, on the client's bill, in terms of place of service. At the time of writing this article, the allowable CPT codes for TMH services include 90832, 90834, 90845, and 90847. In coding the place of service, the current practice is to use the modifier GT—indicating interactive audio and video telecommunication—when billing Medicare, and the modifier 95 when billing commercial insurance companies. The modifier 95 was created in 2017 by the American Medical Association.

It is always a good idea to check whether the client's insurance covers TMH services and document this in the client's record. As of this writing, 31 states and the District of Columbia have enacted laws prohibiting insurers from refusing to cover TMH services if they cover these same services in person. Allowable billing codes for TMH and modifiers change frequently so be sure to check before using them.

9. Thou shalt not Google or friend clients.

What's wrong with Googling, "friending," or establishing other relationships with clients on social media? It is certainly a common practice for patients to Google us or request to friend us. In a recent study, Kolmes and Taube (2011) found that 70% of 333 clients surveyed found personal information about their therapists on the Internet; 87% of these clients did so intentionally; and 72% did not tell their therapists about this.

The mandate against Googling clients, "friending" them, or entering into any relationship on social media is to avoid dual or multiple relationships. It is believed that a dual relationship carries the inherent risks of losing therapist objectivity and effectiveness and may damage the therapeutic relationship. Kaslow, Patterson and Gottlieb (2011, p. 106) warn that an online relationship with a client might lead to the client's perception of the relationship becoming "a more casual or even social one that may violate the boundaries or context of therapy as a sanctuary for exploring personal issues."

Further risks of relationships with clients on social media include breach of client confidentiality and privacy and violation of the trust of the client. An exception to this rule of not Googling clients is Googling them under special circumstances such as when concerned for their safety. These exceptions should be stated in advance in informed consent and processed with the client if they occur.

10. Thou shalt not speak falsely online.

As many therapists now have professional websites, blogs, YouTube videos, Twitter accounts, etc., we are not immune to the dangers of having an online or social media presence. Such dangers might include our falling into self-promotion by false advertising on our website or having clients write reviews/testimonials for us on our website, Yelp, or other review sites. These forms of self-promotion are considered ethical violations. Another danger is our disclosing personal information or views online that might adversely affect our work, our relationship with clients, or damage the reputation of our profession.

The APA Code of Ethics (2017, p. 2) makes a distinction between "psychologists' activities that are part of their scientific, educational, or professional roles as psychologists" and "purely private conduct," which is not in the purview of the ethics code. Likewise, the NASW Code of Ethics (2017, 4.06 Misrepresentation) states that: "Social workers make clear distinctions between statements made and actions engaged in as a private individual and as a representative of the social work profession...." But, in actual practice, how well are we able to make distinctions between our online personal selves and our professional selves? And, if we are having difficulty with this, how savvy do we expect our clients to be in making this distinction? So, the prudent approach may be to strive to have an online presence that, without fail, reflects our honesty and integrity, and willingness to operate within the boundaries of our professional competence and respect for our profession.

In conclusion, the Ten Tech Commandments are to guide you as you navigate both the opportunities and challenges of telemental health practice. To keep pace with our ever-changing technology and ever-developing TMH field, we will need to acquire new knowledge and clinical skills and follow professional TMH standards as they evolve. Under the circumstances, the best advice might be to accept the challenge of keeping up with emerging technology and be open to the significant benefits that new TMH approaches might offer our clients. ▼

References:

American Psychological Association (2013). *APA Guidelines for the Practice of Telepsychology*. Retrieved from: http://www.apapracticecentral.org/ce/guidelines/telepsychology-guidelines.pdf.

American Psychological Association (2017). *American Psychological Association Code of Ethics*. Retrieved from: http://www.apa.org/ethics/code/ethics-code-2017.pdf.

Benton, S. A., Snowden, S. J., & Lee, G. (2016). Therapist-assisted, online (TAO) intervention for anxiety in college students: TAO outperformed treatment as usual. *Professional Psychology: Research and Practice,* 47(5), 363-371.

Harris, E. & Youngren, J.N. (2011). Risk management in the digital world. *Professional Psychology: Research and Practice,* 42(6), 412-418.

Kolmes, K. & Taube, D.O. (2016). Client discovery of psychotherapist personal information online. *Professional Psychology: Research and Practice,* 47(2), 147-154.

Kaslow, F.W., Patterson, T., & Gottlieb, M. (2011). Ethical dilemmas in psychologist accessing internet data: Is it justified? *Professional Psychology: Research and Practice,* 42(2), 105-112.

National Association of Social Workers and Association of Social Work Boards (2005). *Technology and Social Work Practice.* Retrieved from: https://www.aswb.org/wp-content/uploads/2013/10/TechnologySWPractice.pdf.

National Board for Certified Counselors (2016). National Board for Certified Counselors (NBCC) *Policy Regarding the Provision of Distance Practice.* Retrieved from: http://www.nbcc.org/Assets/Ethics/NBCCPolicyRegardingPracticeofDistanceCounselingBoard.pdf.

National Center for Telehealth and Technology (2011). *Introduction to Telemental Health.* Retrieved from: http://t2health.dcoe.mil/sites/default/files/cth/introduction/intro_telemental_health_may2011.pdf.

Implements and Weapons: Children, Teens and Digital Media

Penelope Norton

PENELOPE NORTON, PhD, practices psychology in Ormond Beach, Florida. She provides psychotherapy to children, teens, adults, couples, families and seniors. Her 35 years of practice have brought her increasing confidence and humility. She is inspired by Ralph Waldo Emerson, who wrote, "What lies behind us and what lies before us are tiny matters compared to what lies within us."
psynorton@aol.com

One can imagine cave-dweller parents with the discovery of fire: "Look, kids! Hot food!" And, "Stay back! Adults only!" With the advent of the forge and steel, agrarian parents faced similar dilemmas about knives or axes or plows. Each step of progress with implements introduced more steps requiring caution, protection and supervision of children.

Growing up in the 1950s and '60s, I was not allowed to own a jackknife until age 10. Before then, the jackknife was for adults only. And, in a similar vein, I progressed from rounded paper scissors, to pointed paper scissors, to adult scissors, and lastly to sewing scissors, a sacred tool in our home. Each step toward independent use of tools was imbued with patience, responsibility and pride, as well as with adult protection. In fact, the use of most everyday household tools required respect and care of the implements. My father's toolbox was off limits without permission and/or supervision, as was my mother's sewing machine. Their tools and implements were expensive and deserving of care; the list of implements to which the proper attitude was extended included garden tools, kitchen equipment, and entertainment devices such as record players, radios, the television and telephone. The tools of our age are electronic devices, evoking the same parental delight and consternation as the implement advances of earlier generations.

As a parent, I have had my challenges and victories with the use of electronics. In the most concerning incident, when one son was about seven, I called him to dinner. Eventually, on the second nag, he yelled, "Well, I'll just have to kill myself, then." Of course, all my mental health provider fears kicked in, until my other son explained that it meant *stopping* in the early edition of *Super Mario* (Nintendo, 1985), requiring the player to start the game completely anew. In a later incident, when one teen son was staying up late using what was then the family computer, he claimed to be completely mystified as to why we were flooded with spam porn. On the other hand, the free online math tutoring of Kahn Academy was a lifesaver for two of my children in high school, providing a service I could neither offer nor afford myself. My teen daughter and her friends benefitted from the Dove Self Esteem (Unilever, 2004) project and its debunking of stereotyped and unrealistic body images portrayed in media. Family media experiences have been both friend and foe to my children.

At my office, I have always required respect for the playroom toys and their use. In particular, the sandtray toys have a dedicated purpose, and are off limits for other forms of play. The waiting-room toys are designed to evoke busy work rather than inner work and help maintain the boundary and differentiation of the two tasks. For example, word searches, mazes, puzzles and books occupy clients in the waiting room without evoking much about the purpose of a child's visit with me. I have written elsewhere about some of the specifics of playroom set-up and play room toys, as well as sandtray (Norton, 2012). I do not allow electronic toys in the playroom, to the consternation of some patients. But, I set more flexible boundaries with teens who are ready for "talk" therapy. As a psychologist and therapist to children and teens, I am often confronted with them bearing electronics and with the dilemmas of their parents regarding the place of these tools in their family life. My patients, their parents and I have grown together in exploring their uses, both in their homes, and in my office. Some uses of these new tools with children and teens were unimaginable only a few years ago. And, the new tools are applicable to wide ranges of clinical problems and developmental ages.

For a time, I received many calls to treat attention deficit disorder (with or without hyperactivity) without medication. This was in line with my preference for trying non-medication interventions first, especially with pre-teen children. Both Lumosity (Lumos Labs, Inc., 2005) and Journey to Wild (Unyte, 2001) are commercially available programs that report that they strengthen, memory, focus and attention. A recent American Psychologist article (Thibault, R. and Raz, A. (2017), reported that neurofeedback (specifically EEG feedback) derived most of its benefits from placebo effects. And, this may also be true of other commercial products, even expensive treatments such as Cog Med (Pearson Education, Inc., 1998). However, when parents work with their children using one of these programs, the attachment time sitting next to one another is very calming for the child, improves their relationship, and makes all of them feel less helpless, even when the gains are modest. That combined with education for the parents and with other strategies is often enough for meaningful improvement, even if medication may be required at some later point.

For teens with anxiety disorders, the advantages of the digital age are enormous. I have numerous teens and adults with anxiety disorders who utilize Headspace (Headspace, 2010) or Calm (Calm.com, Inc., 2012) as both mindfulness and anxiety-reduction training. Not only do my patients learn these skills, but they have the resource immediately available to them in the moments when their anxiety levels spike, sometimes even in the classroom. They are empowered to help themselves, which also lessens their anxiety. And, with teens, they are in control of their use of the product, which reduces their opposition to it. Further, many of my teens have downloaded Marconi's musical composition "Weightless" (the 10-hour version) on their phones, a product with the ability to lower anxiety by 60% in users (Gillett, 2016). Finally, commercially available audio anxiety-reduction products, such as "The Ten Minute Stress Manager" (Miller, 1997), or "Letting Go of Stress" (Drmiller.com, 2003), can be downloaded directly from iTunes (Apple Computer, 2001) in my office: no waiting, no sending someone home to order a product, no forgetting, accidentally or oppositionally.

Both Headspace (Headspace, 2010) and Here Comes a Thought (Sugar, R., 2016) are useful as treatments for depression. They emphasize staying in the moment, reducing rumination and increasing mindfulness. In my experience, all of these reduce depression-related outbursts of aggression in teens, including cyber-aggression, and help those teens develop an ability to protect themselves from their own impulses.

Digital devices are also very helpful in improving sleep onset in both children and teens who struggle with this. Commercial audio sleep products, such as Easing into Sleep (Miller, 1996), contribute skills and a sense of control that speed resolution, because these products are available in the moment and can be controlled by the teen or by a parent for a child.

The Fisher Wallace Stimulator (Fisher Wallace Laboratories, 2007) has been shown to reduce insomnia by 60%, depression by 50%. It treats anxiety and pain as well. It works by electromagnetic stimulation and is easily used by clients at home for approximately 20 minutes per day. I have a couple patients who have significantly reduced insomnia by using it. The stimulator can be used as an adjunct to medication, or, for some people, as an alternative to medication (Levine, 2016).

Finally, digital media help me know and attach to all my clients better. They easily bring photos of themselves with friends (or without friends, to portray their loneliness). They can show me projects from science or art of which they are proud, Facebook or other bullying experiences that hurt them, and aspects of their family life or home I might not otherwise know; as they say, sometimes a picture is worth a thousand words. I do allow teens with ambivalent attachment issues to email/text to my email, which comes to my phone. We discuss this with some ground rules, but usually, knowing that they are *allowed* to contact me provides the secure attachment that they need, and I am rarely contacted.

Currently, a transgender teen is showing me his plans for his future look, which provides us concrete information in real time of his rejection of the girl that he has been, and his hope for his future. This same teen also shows me photos of his beloved cats, a source of comfort and companionship in his difficult world.

My interaction with children and teens regarding electronics also allows me to engage with them in gentle competition; for example, they like to find products on their own that are superior to the ones I recommended. They can tease me about my age-deficiency in electronic use. Sometimes they advise me on products I should consider, "to help other kids." Teens gain particular strength in small victories with adults, especially in a society that seems to tell them that they must wait to contribute. They take from these moments a greater sense of purpose. Often, they are the teachers of parents and elders in the use of electronic devices. Being instructors is an antidote to the barrage of instruction they receive every day. They like to be needed and to have their contributions acknowledged.

Overall, digital media are the new world of my young patients, and I want to join them in it.

So, what about the dangers?

First, some cautionary tales from my caseload:

Six-year-old Max was brought in by his parents for "hyperactivity," as diagnosed by his teachers. Max was bright, energetic and filled with ambivalence for his younger sister. His parents were educated, conscientious people. However, Max knew a LOT about sex, and it frightened him. His projective testing and play were also filled with content about the need to protect himself from adult men and from anger. He seemed to have negative feelings about his maternal grandfather, who, the mother reported, had been suspected of sexually abusing her niece. The parents wanted to know who had hurt Max and decided to keep Max away from unsupervised contact with his grandfather for a while. Max never disclosed any names of perpetrators, and I never felt that an abuser was identified. However, Max was also obsessed with the video game *Minecraft* (MojangAB, 2009). With support from his parents for his anxieties, specific "body privacy" training, and months of play therapy, Max's anxiety and distress decreased. Not long after, his parents discovered that there were *Minecraft* links to adult pornography accessible to children. The parents learned how to disable the links, and Max's anxiety decreased still further. When I stopped seeing Max, family repercussions about their limits with the grandfather were still causing distress, although it seemed that the *Minecraft* links were the cause of his acute distress. Those links not only injured Max but also harmed Max's relationships with his parents, teacher, and grandparents.

Thirteen-year-old Mary was the picture of a young adolescent. She was plump, awkwardly developing with heavy facial acne and greasy hair. She arrived in my office in hysterical tears, having been "dragged" to the visit by her angry parents. Needing to feel attractive, Mary had taken naked photos of herself for a middle-school boy, who she hoped would find her attractive and "maybe even" like her. Although she did not share the photos with anyone else, he shared them with "a couple of people." Apparently, her naked body was shown to any number of Eastern European men who were continually contacting her with explicit sexual requests and content. Mary's wounded sexuality and shame from the photo-sharing and from her parents felt to her unbearable.

Jenna, a slightly older 14-year-old girl, had been diagnosed with attention deficit disorder. This diagnosis was given at her age eight by a local psychologist who specialized in ADD. Jenna had been prescribed several different medications to control her overactive behavior and lack of impulse control. Jenna had been adopted at birth by a kind, educated couple. Like many adoptees, at puberty she became interested in her birth family. She located her birth mother online and began a correspondence with this local woman, who was eager to claim her long-lost child and insert herself into Jenna's life. The adoptive parents were initially supportive of this "surprise" turn of events but became alarmed as they discovered Jenna's birth mother led a very chaotic life due to her bipolar disorder. The discovery of her birth mother's life was very disappointing to Jenna, although it ultimately led to Jenna's diagnosis with bipolar disorder. This series of events occurred before Jenna was emotionally prepared to process and accept the discoveries she made.

Recently, two five-year-old boys have been my patients. One of them was expelled from his kindergarten because he threatened to "duct tape" a classmate into a closet and then "blow his head off." When questioned by his teacher, this boy reported that he had learned this from his mother, which led to a child abuse report. Ultimately, it emerged that the boy and his young mother watched and played a lot of videogames. This child, from his screen time, had a clinically significant trauma profile as measured by the Trauma Symptom Checklist for Young Children (TSCYC, Briere, 2005).

The second five-year-old is filled with aggression, displayed at home and at school. In my playroom he played out numerous scenes of military-type violence. In discussing the protagonist of his play enactments, he related that "heroes fight." When asked, he could identify no other behavior of heroes, such as protection of another, rescue of another, or other more pro-social goals of heroes worshipped by five-year-olds. This boy, from an affluent family, has his own videogame console in his room, with unrestricted use.

These specific case stories were unheard of a generation ago. And, daily, I see more pedestrian problems of technology in my office, such as sleep deprivation due to video-gaming or use of cell phones in the beds of children and teens, weight gain due to lack of exercise, and reduced interaction time with parents or peers due to the solitary nature of electronic use.

Broader Concerns

We already know that exposure to video and movie violence begets violence:

> The relationship between media violence and real-life aggression is easily as strong as the impact of cigarette smoking on lung cancer. Not everyone who smokes will get lung cancer, and not everyone who views media violence will become aggressive themselves. However, the connection is significant. The most problematic forms of media violence include attractive and unpunished perpetrators, no harm to victims, realism and humor (American Academy of Pediatrics, Committee on Public Health, 2001).

We already know that the lack of green time leads to weight gain and disconnection with our mothership, the Earth (Luov, 2008). Less known, however, is the impact of electronics on the development of the capacity for connection and empathy. The impact of light exposure on the increased incidence of mood disorder is only beginning to be known. And, further, the impacts of electromagnetic exposure on human development generally, and on brain health specifically, have received little attention in the popular (non-scientific) press.

In our offices, daily, we see the negative impact on families and relationships that can be caused by impaired capacity for empathy. Presumably, empathic impairments have remained relatively stable across recent decades. However, current neuroscience research provides data on the development of mirror neurons; they develop through "'monkey see, monkey do,' or 'peek-a boo,'" type interactions (Williams, Whiten, Suddendorf and Perrett, 2001, p.10). From literature on botox and on Parkinson's disease (Neal, D. and Chartrand, T., 2011), we know that when motor memory in human interaction is impaired, empathy declines. Psychologist David Paltin (2007, p. 2) asks, "Will the amount of time kids spend looking at a glowing screen change the way mirror neurons activate? Will we shut off a real quality of empathy and connection when we let them [children] interact more with screens than with other humans?" This is of particular concern given that we know there are critical periods for neurological development of some skills, and that skills, when learned, can we be lost without use. For example, musical skills require activation before age nine, foreign language skills are best learned before age seven (Neerguard, 2009). From my understanding of developmental psychology, the most vulnerable ages for this type of impairment would seem to be in early-to-mid childhood, yet screen time is increasing for younger and younger children.

Within our society, mood disorders seem to be increasing, and reliance on anti-depressant medication in our population is sometimes as high as 30%. Research by Michael Terman and his colleagues (Terman, M. and McMahan, I., 2012) has shown that the incidence of mood disorders increases with exposure to blue light and reduction in natural light. This same increase in mood disorders is also related to sleep deprivation, fueled by the same over-exposure to the blue-spectrum light of screens. Research by Twenge and her colleagues (Twenge, Joiner, Rogers, and Martin, 2017), with a sample size of a half million adolescents, documents that increases in depressive symptoms and suicide are linked to increased screen use. We also know that earlier exposure to depression leads to a greater lifetime incidence of depressive episodes. Presumably, then, as younger and younger children are exposed to earlier and earlier screen time, incidence of depression will likely rise.

Last, what do we know about the long-term effects of exposure to wifi and electromagnetic fields? As early as 2004, a relationship was discovered between screen time in early childhood and subsequent attentional problems in children (Christakis, Zimmerman, DiGiuseppe, and McCarty, 2004). But, is the increasing incidence of attention deficit disorders simply the screen time, is it partly caused by electromagnetic exposure, or both? Pall (2016) summarizes the neuropsychiatric effect of non-thermal electromagnetic radiation (EMF) based on occupational and epidemiological studies. Commonly reported neuropsychiatric changes include sleep disturbance, headache, depression, concentration and attention dysfunction, memory changes, EEG changes and more. The impact of EMF on children and teens is magnified due to their less-developed and smaller-sized brains. Pall reports data connecting higher number of cell-phone calls with increased incidence of attention deficit disorder. Of still greater concern is the list of countries that limit EMF exposures: Denmark, Finland, France, Germany, India, Israel, Switzerland, Turkey, Canada, *but not the United States* (Redmayne, 2015).

Child psychiatrist Victoria Dunckley, author of *Re-Set Your Child's Brain: A Four Week Plan to End Meltdowns, Raise Grades and Boost Social Skills by Reversing the Effects of Electronic Screen Time* (2015), provides an integrated perspective of electronic media on children's health. She proposes electronic screen syndrome (ESS), a comprehensive diagnosis caused by excessive electronic stimulation. She presents data to show that screen time induces stress, activates the child's reward pathways so that they require more and more stimulation, and impairs cognition and learning. She includes the following symptoms of ESS: dysregulated mood; impaired cognition focus and memory; and behavioral dysfunction including oppositional-defiant behavior and low empathy. She further argues that the stress response induced by ESS decreases blood flow to the frontal lobe and results in poor frontal-lobe development and functioning. She documents the exacerbation of mood disorders, ADHD, anxiety disorders and autistic spectrum disorders in children with ESS and has been able to improve psychiatric functioning and reduce psychiatric medication by placing children on an electronic fast. Max, Mary, Jenna and my two five-year-old patients are all represented by Dunckley's comprehensive perspective.

How can we help?

My concern with child advocacy started early in my life. A classmate and friend in elementary school, Dana, had only one arm, having been born a "thalidomide baby" before the dangers of the "new tool" were brought to public awareness. As mental health providers on the front lines of intake and treatment, I believe we are in unique positions to observe the "canaries in the coal mine," the cognitive and mental health impact on our children and teens related to electronic media and screen time.

On a micro level, we can inform parents and grandparents about the risk factors of screen time. I have had some successes in reducing screen time for my young patients. I have been able to improve sleep and mood in numerous teens by using blue light-blocking glasses, along with reduction of screen time. I have been able to encourage some teens to listen to material before sleep (such as stories or relaxation materials) rather than going to sleep with their cell phones or televisions on. I encourage parents of children under 14 to store and charge cell phones out of children's bedrooms at night, and I regularly object to televisions located in children's bedrooms. I recently recommended that a young mother not enroll her child in a preschool located beneath a cell tower.

On a larger scale, in my community, when I have an opportunity to teach groups of parents through community lectures, I can reach a broader audience. Opportunities to teach other professionals, including teachers, family practice physicians, and child-care providers, also increase awareness on a broader scale. For recommendations regarding screen time for children and adolescents, I refer my audiences to the guidelines published by the American College of Pediatricians (Anderson, 2016), to the Environmental Health Trust, and, of course, to Dunckley's (2015) work.

On yet a larger scale, I have become more politically active. We must elect politicians and policy-makers who fund the science needed when new products are introduced, and who rely on that science for policy decisions that protect our future generations. ▼

References:

American Academy of Pediatrics, Committee on Public Education. (2001). Media violence. *Pediatrics.* 108(5):1222-1226.

Anderson, J. (2016) The impact of media use and screen time on children, adolescents and families. American College of Pediatricians.

Apple Computer, Inc. (2001). iTunes. Cupertino, CA.

Briere, J. (2005). Trauma Symptom Checklist for Young Children. Odessa, FL Psychological Asssessment Resources (PAR, Inc.).

Calm.com, Inc. (2012). Calm. San Francisco, CA.

Christakis, D., Zimmerman, F., DiGiuseppe, D., & McCarty, C. (2004). Early television exposure and subsequent attentional problems in children. *Pediatrics.* 113:708-713.

Dunckley, V. (2015) *Re-set your child's brain: A four week plan to end meltdowns, raise grades, and boost social skills by reversing the effects of screen time.* Novato, CA: New World Library.

Fisher Wallace Laboratories (2007). Fisher Wallace Stimulator. New York.

Gillett, R. (2016). The song to listen to if you want to significantly reduce your anxiety in less than 10 minutes. Retrieved from: www.businessinsider.com/the-song-that-could-reduce-your-anxiety-in-less-than-10-minutes-2016-11.

Halpern, S. & Miller, E. (2003). Letting go of stress. Drmiller.com, Nevada City, CA.

Headspace (2010). Headspace. Santa Monica, CA.

Levine, D. (2016). Why I get my brain zapped. Retrieved from: Blogs.scientificamerican.com/mind-guest-blog/why-i-get-my-brain-zapped.

Lumos Labs, Inc. (2005). Lumosity. San Francisco, CA.

Luov, R. (2008). *Last child in the woods: Saving our children from nature-deficit disorder.* Chapel Hill, NC: Algonquin Books.

Marconi Union (2014). Ambient Transmissions, volume 2. Weightless (official 10-hour version). London: Just Music.

Miller, E. (1996). Easing into sleep. Hay House audio. Carlsbad, CA.

Miller, E. (1997). The 10 minute stress manager. Hay House audio. Carlsbad, CA.

MojangAB (2009). Minecraft. Stockholm, Sweden.

Neal, D. & Chartrand, T. (2011). Embodied emotion perception: Amplifying and dampening facial feedback modulates emotional perception accuracy. *Social Psychological and Personality Sciences.* 2, 673-678.

Neerguard, L. (07/20/2009). Language best learned by age 7, study shows. *Newsday.*

Nintendo (1985). Super Mario Brothers. Kyoto, Japan.

Norton, P. (2012). Swimming upstream. *Voices* 48:3 p.7-21.

Pall, M. (2016). Microwave frequency electromagnetic fields (EMFs) produce widespread neuropsychiatric effects including depression. *Journal of Chemical Neuroanatomy* 75 (Pt B) 43-51.

Paltin, D. (2012). Mirror, mirror in the brain—reflections on the "talking twins." Child Development Institute. Orange, CA.

PearsonEducation, Inc. (1998). CogMed. London, UK.

Redmayne, M. (2015). International policy and advisory response regarding children's exposure to radiofrequency electromagnetic fields (RF-EMF). *Electromagnetic Biology and Medicine.* 35:2, 176-185. DOI 10:3109/15368378.2015.1038832

Sugar, R. (2016). Steven Universe. Here comes a thought. Cartoon Network Studios, Burbank, CA.

Terman, M. & McMahan, I. (2012). *Chronotherapy: Resetting your inner clock to boost mood, alertness, and quality sleep.* New York: Avery.

Thibault, R. & Raz, A. (2017). The psychology of neurofeedback. *American Psychologist* 72:7, 679-687.

Twenge, J., Joiner, T., Rogers, M. & Martin, G. (2017). *Clinical Psychological Science,* 6:1, 3-17. Doi.org/10.1177/2167702617723376.

Unilever (2004). Dove Soap. Dove Self Esteem Project. Englewood Cliffs, NJ.

Williams, J, Whiten, A., Suddendorf, T. & Perrett, D. (2001). Imitation, mirror neurons and autism. *Neuroscience and Behavioral Reviews.* 25:4 287-295.

Campbell States

Is Social Media the New Imaginary Audience?

CAMPBELL STATES, LICSW, practices in downtown Washington, DC. She is in her second year of membership in the American Academy of Psychotherapists. Campbell received her MSS from Bryn Mawr College and recently completed a two-year certificate program in psychodynamic psychotherapy from the Institute of Contemporary Psychotherapy and Psychoanalysis. In her free time, she enjoys oil painting and Kundalini yoga.
Campbell.States@gmail.com

MY CLIENT MINDY IS A 28-YEAR-OLD WOMAN WHO NEEDS TO BE PERFECT. She came to therapy because her life was not perfect. She feels empty and unfulfilled at work. She is tearful as she tells me she left her family and moved across the country to join her long-distance boyfriend of five years and then realized the relationship was over. Mindy tells me about screaming fights over the dishes and engaging in self-destructive behaviors to recover her equilibrium afterwards. Then she looks through her phone, finds an image of a happier time, a picture of her and her partner being cute, and posts it online. Mindy uses social media to post about their relationship. Despite her ongoing struggles, Mindy only posts content that shows a fun, carefree and exciting life.

Liz, another client, is a thoughtful and serious 25-year-old woman. She started therapy in the aftermath of a difficult break-up. While with her partner, Liz had been a frequent consumer of social media, but had never posted anything on her accounts. In fact, with her partner, Liz had agreed that she preferred not to use social media. After a few months of processing feelings of grief and guilt associated with the relationship, Liz was beginning to re-build a sense of identity without her partner. Liz arrived agitated one day. She said she had written a blog post that she wanted to share with her friends and felt confused about whether post it on Facebook. We explored her feelings in greater depth. They focused on one anxiety, "Am I a person who uses social media?"

Although it seems clear social media provides a new arena for development and is incorporated into adolescent grappling with the developmental task of individuation, social media is also an aspect of contemporary adult life with observable connections to the tangible world. In 1967, psychologist David Elkind coined the term "imaginary audience," referring to a state of mind in which an individual believes that those around him, even people he does not know, are closely watching him with intense interest. This usually happens during adolescence. Elkind states, "The adolescent is continually constructing, or reacting to an imaginary audience. It is an audience because the adolescent believes that he will be the focus of attention; and imaginary because, in actual social situations this is usually not the case (unless he contrives to make it so)" (1967, p. 1030). Elkind theorized that this adolescent egocentrism, where the adolescent projects all his great anxieties about himself onto those around him and imagines they are as preoccupied with his sense of identity as he, is a normal stage of development and is the source of the acute self-consciousness of adolescents.

Social media is a digital space where people can share content including information, ideas, personal messages and images to others in their network. The most popular social media sites include Facebook, Twitter and Instagram. While social media users frequently speak about an "online community," some social media interactions involve communication with, to, or from strangers or online acquaintances, while others involve communication with family members and others social media users know in real life (IRL). Before social media, the evidence of the imaginary audience was found in the interactions of adolescents with their families, peers, and the larger society of their town or city. As social media has developed, adolescents who are grappling with the imaginary audience can also be observed in social media interactions. However, beyond the imaginary audience, social media has created a space in which adult interactions also occur and have real world impact.

Elkind (1967) reasoned that the resolution of this developmental stage was through the development of "intimacy" as conceived by Eric Erickson. According to Erickson, intimacy is the process by which the adolescent is able to see himself more clearly by entering into a relationship based on mutuality with others. In the process of connection, he becomes able to understand his real—rather than imagined—impact on others and discovers that others have experienced the suffering he has (in Elkind, p. 1032). In the case of my client Mindy, use of social media is an extension of the imagined audience past an average age where many have moved from this adolescent perspective toward the more mature relational process of intimacy. Mindy's use of social media reflects a larger clinical issue, where she is disavowing parts of herself in real-world and digital presentation. Mindy almost exclusively views herself through the lens of an imagined other. In therapy she is working on exploring and accepting the parts of herself that are less perfect. In this process she is hoping to gain a greater sense of intimacy with herself and others. In the case of Liz, she appears to view social media use as an aspect of life she can re-examine now that her partner is gone. She is also attempting to reintegrate parts of herself she gave up to be in a relationship. Social media is now the arena where the invisible audience watches its young (and old) players. However, the process and need to find intimacy in order to become our whole selves remains the same. We need to connect. ▼

References:
Elkind, D. (1967). Egocentrism in adolescence. *Child Development, 38*(4), pp. 1025-1034. DOI: 10.2307/1127100

Erin McCarthy

Text Me When You Get Here: Allowing Technology in the Therapeutic Playroom

THE BRIGHT TOYS AND CURIOUS OBJECTS THAT LIVE IN MY PLAYROOM/OFFICE INVITE TOUCH AND EXPLORATION: an Oscar the Grouch beanbag, the perfect size for throwing; smooth shells that prompt the question, "Are these real?"; the silky tresses of a pink-haired doll; thousands of multicolored beads and stickers.

One object doesn't do much of anything—it's incredibly ordinary, and yet hums with power—its value immeasurable. It's an old, intact iPhone 4 I found while cleaning out the closet in my apartment, long discarded and deemed worthless by a former roommate. In my playroom, completely uncharged and dead, it is still charged with projections and potential.

The word "phone" doesn't fully express or describe the capabilities of this device. It's a dictionary, encyclopedia, vision board, gaming center, portal to friends and strangers, book, flashlight, sound maker, music player, broadcaster.

The original play therapists—Anna Freud, Melanie Klein and Donald Winnicott, to name a few—didn't have such a powerful vehicle with which to both stimulate and enact inner conflicts and responses to the environment. Klein's play therapy protocol specified a box filled with a few simple items: a string, a few neutral figures, a baby doll. My first supervisors recalled times in which play therapy didn't involve crafts or Barbies or board games, nostalgically idealizing a simpler time.

My philosophy is different: rather than providing a neutral place and simple toys, I bring stimulating materials that aim to spark recognition, connection, discussion, or something unknown. While I suspected an old iPhone would generate these states, I've been astonished by how it allows children to share their experience of inhabiting

ERIN MCCARTHY, MSW, practices psychotherapy with children, adolescents and adults in the Dupont Circle neighborhood of Washington, DC. She was a "scholar" at AAP's 2016 Institute & Conference, and is renewed, refreshed and stimulated by her burgeoning connection with AAP, having attended the last two Southern Region conferences as well as the Mid-Atlantic salons and workshops. When not reading, writing, thinking or talking about psychotherapy, she enjoys painting, printmaking, adventuring and cooking.
erin.elizabeth.mccarthy@gmail.com

this technologically-connected world. Technology impacts life and so impacts the therapeutic encounter, particularly with young minds whose only world is the present one. In this article, I will present several case examples that illustrate the power and impact of technology on the young mind as presented in the therapeutic playroom.

An 11-year-old client slips the phone into her back pocket with casual ease. She doesn't have a phone of her own, but she can have this one, if only for 45 minutes. Our reciprocal play story of her own imagining features me as a girl, hapless at making friends, who's been tricked into drinking vomit. As the trick is played, she films me with the phone. "You just drank vomit," she states with contempt. I play up my disgust, "vomiting" myself. With practiced ease, she films the moment and posts it for all to see. "It's posted." She prompts me to cry in embarrassment while she laughs cruelly. Later, after the story is over and the session is ending, she pleads with me to let her take something from my playroom with her to school, where she has trouble making friends and feels unaccepted. The play story comes full circle, with the phone a channel to portraying her inner conflicts—her experiences of being shamed and publicly ridiculed.

Dr. Laura Markham, a popular therapist whose work is grounded in attachment theory, relays that many children report that the most important thing in their parents' lives is their phone (Markham, 2017). My friends and colleagues with babies and young children note how their kids gravitate toward it, trying to touch it or hold it or press its little button, which lights it up. The importance of the phone sparks varied reactions in parents ranging from apprehension to dismissiveness, reactions which I've seen continue and transform throughout the childhood lifespan. Parents wonder, when is the right time to let my child use a phone? Have her own phone? Go on social media?

Several dynamics emerge from these questions—the idea that children want to use the phone and we must protect them from it; the idea that the phone can expose children to a terrifying and inappropriate world from which they optimally should be shielded; the idea that once the child has a phone, he or she is forever lost to the swirling and treacherous waters of technology. Again, we revisit the idea of childhood "innocence"—a nostalgic, unreliable projection that impairs our seeing each child for who he or she is: a real person with real feelings and an emerging ability to consent. My experience with adolescents shows that each one has a varied interest in technology. The prevalence and ubiquity of it all, though, adds a certain pressure to the challenges of growing up.

One girl, a 12-year-old interested in crafts, fashion and other expressions of her identity, engaged in a power struggle with her admittedly Luddite parents around granting her access to Instagram. Already experiencing social challenges at school, she wanted to meet her classmates in this arena and connect with others who might share her interests. S had recently received a diagnosis of autism spectrum disorder, which gave some context to highly specific and strong interests and challenges in social communication. Her mother's refusal to allow her access to a world in which she perceived she could connect with other kids like her was a perpetual source of conflict and misunderstanding.

I identify as a "millennial" in that I grew up with technology. I had a computer in grade school and was lurking in chat rooms as early as age 9. My parents' lax supervision dovetailed with unprecedented access to information and connection through AOL in the late 1990s, and I spent many nights connecting with people, known and unknown, across the Internet. In high school, procrastination and crushes and conflicts played out on my computer screen, with away-messages that said just enough to (hopefully) be read as meaningful and intriguing. The questions of identity, connection and belonging were so present for me as I interacted with technology as a young teen. I struggled to feel accepted in my suburban middle and high schools, but online I could follow my curiosity without such self-consciousness. I could identify with S's struggle.

Another 12-year-old girl declared to me each session that she was not into social media. I asked her if that was a problem.

V: I don't really like social media. I'm like, not on Instagram or Snapchat, but all of my classmates are.
E: Is that a problem for you?
V: Maybe? Like, I feel kind of disconnected, but I also don't like social media so.... I don't really talk to my classmates outside of school.
E: Do you miss them when you're not there?
V: Not really.
E: You've said before that you're introverted—maybe you get enough contact at school and when you're at home, you're just connecting with yourself and your family.
V: Maybe...

She became distracted, looking at a penny she found in her pocket. It was from the year 1985, and I disclosed that I was born that year, which I like because it makes my age easy to calculate. She agreed, and we discovered we're almost exactly 20 years apart—she was born in 2005. I shared with her my impression that social media might make being in middle school harder—about my suburban childhood in which my mom would drop me off at the mall for a few hours, completely unsupervised, without a phone. This girl's mother allowed her to enter the door of my building and required a text from her when she arrived in my office, which she sometimes forgot to send. I'd then receive a text—had she arrived? Yes. I told V that I only had to know what time to meet my mother outside the mall and that, other than using my phone card to call her, there was no other way to get in touch.

V: I think I would rather have grown up when you did.

We assume that children must be protected from the phone and social media, but what about the effects of technology on us, the parents and adults in their lives? The ability to constantly check in, to text if we're late, to be in touch, to be tethered—to not assume that the person with whom we are in relationship is ok unless they respond immediately, to need that reassuring message. I wonder how this affects trust, attachment and security in young people today. They are sure to let me know.

In play therapy, I see and experience the effects of these dynamics through reciprocal play. In a session with a 7-year-old girl whose mother proudly identified as a workaholic, I was on the receiving end of the vacant gaze and distraction she must have experienced in relationship with her mother.

L: Ok, let's pretend. I'm the mom and you're the kid. Try to talk to me, try to tell me something about your day at school.

E: Ok. So, today at school…
L: (Eyes downcast, tapping furiously at the phone.) Mmmhmmm.
E: Um, I played with my friend Alice, she wanted to run around on the playground but I…
L: What? Hold on… (tapping at phone). Keep talking.
E: Well, I wanted to read instead, but I wasn't sure if she would still be my friend.
L: Oh, sorry, I have a call. (Answers phone.) Yes? Yes… oh yeah, I'll get that to you right away.

I felt discouraged, hopeless and annoyed—through play, she let me know what it was like to be her, interacting with a preoccupied, unavailable mother.

Many clinicians are familiar with the still-face experiment. In 1975, Dr. Edward Tronick presented a study featuring a mother-baby dyad in which for three minutes, the mother presents a "still" or blank face to a baby making bids for connection. The video invokes a sense of despair in the viewer as the baby exhibits preoccupation, then discouragement, as she is unsuccessful in her attempts to establish a here-and-now emotional reciprocity. The baby eventually withdraws, averts her gaze and body away from the mother and takes on a zoned-out expression, dissociating from this disturbing reality. While misattunement is nothing new, the phone and its seductive promise to attune to our every desire, often unstated, presents a new challenge for the parent-child relationship and as such, the therapist-patient relationship.

I worked for three years with a mysterious child, L, who was nonverbal in session for more than half of the treatment, taking place from 7-10 years of age. My own process during this treatment was tortured—I hated tolerating my own discomfort, lack of control and inability to woo him into connection. This was my first position out of graduate school, and I felt driven to prove myself. After a year, he began to communicate with me through writing, sharing that he didn't know why he didn't want to talk—he just didn't. We played *Chutes and Ladders* endlessly—with L pointing to each picture, prompting me to explain the cause-and-effect, punishment-and-reward scenarios depicted in the game. "The boy doesn't do his homework, so he has to sit in detention." "The girl reaches up for the cookie jar, but it's too heavy for her and it breaks." One day, he brought his tablet device into the waiting room. It seemed important for him to bring it into the session room, and so he did. He showed me an app called Talking Tom, in which a person speaks into the device and an animated tomcat speaks it back. L finally vocalized during this session, making all kinds of animal sounds which were echoed back to us. My heart melted with relief. While L never became a big talker, he became more and more comfortable relating with me through speech and writing, especially with the aid of technology. I felt comfortable setting limits—we had to play together, it had to be mutual to use the iPad—but I deeply respected his use of technology to break the silence between us.

Another 7-year-old client pleaded with his mother to let him bring his iPad into our session. "Do you allow iPads in session?" she asked, and I felt a strong pull to align with her and say, "No, never, no technology." Perhaps that would make something easier, if we had firm rules around it, or an all-out ban, protecting all of us from the ambiguity of considering each situation, reinforcing the delusion that we can control others. I was curious about what he wanted to show me and said so. "I want to show you my world," he responded. Well, that seemed very important.

We sat next to each other on the couch as he led me through his virtual space, painstakingly created, block by block. I've tried to build my own *Minecraft* world, younger kids laughing as I struggled to push the right buttons to create the most basic of structures. They whizzed around me, building gorgeous floating palaces, coordinating their motor skills and imaginations effortlessly. My blocks stayed scattered, as if my house had been destroyed by the big bad wolf. I felt a rush of fear and resonance as I recognized for the first time what it feels like to be left behind, technologically.

As someone whose later childhood and adolescence were shaped by the connecting and disconnecting qualities of technology, I trust in my ability to challenge and attempt to hold the anxieties and fear that drive adults to ban or prohibit access to technology for children and young adolescents. A key part of my use of technology in the playroom is that it is related, or in relationship. There is a showing or being-seen aspect to it that mirrors being heard, noticed and acknowledged in a more traditional therapeutic sense. To deny technology is to deny part of a child's world, especially if "everyone else" is permitted to engage. While I feel protective of children, I also believe in their capacity to choose what inspires them and begin to hear an inner voice, follow a sense of self-direction and be able to connect with like-minded others. The varied experiences I have had with technology in the playroom and in my own life illustrate that each individual negotiates his or her own relationship and comfort level with technology in his or her own life. I believe in integrating this experience into therapeutic treatment, thanks to the children and adolescents who continually make a case for this openness through play and talk.▼

References

Markham, L. (2017). 10 simple ways to improve your parenting. Retrieved from: http://www.ahaparenting.com/blog/easy-ways-to-improve-your-parenting-no-resolutions-necessary.

Tronick, E., Adamson, L.B., Als, H., & Brazelton, T.B. (1975, April). Infant emotions in normal and perturbated interactions. Paper presented at the biennial meeting of the Society for Research in Child Development, Denver, CO.

Technology and Attunement

Eileen Dombo

I HAVE BEEN TEACHING CLINICAL SOCIAL WORK PRACTICE FOR 15 YEARS AND PRACTICING AS A CLINICIAN FOR OVER 20. When I sat in classrooms during both my MSW and PhD programs, a student using a computer to take notes was rare. I have a vivid memory of two peers in the PhD program—I'll call them James and Joseph—getting into an argument over the noise made by Joseph's laptop computer. James was having trouble hearing the professor over the whining sound emanating from the device, and he was getting more and more agitated as class went on. His emotional state was exacerbated by Joseph's lack of attention to the non-verbal cues of his classmates; he could not see them because he was sitting away from the group, close to the wall (to be near the outlet where his computer was plugged in), staring intently at the screen. James erupted with frustration when he could bear it no longer. What ensued was a lively debate over whether or not we should be using computers in the classroom. I never used a computer in class to take notes and only purchased a laptop computer when it came time to write my dissertation. Now, screens large and small are everywhere I turn. It makes me wonder, can we teach future clinicians to pay close attention and be attuned to clients when people are more connected to a screen than a person?

Not a class session goes by without me looking out to the group of students only to find, not their eyes eager to learn, but the tops of their heads as they stare into their laps. Are they hoping I don't see them checking their phones? "You're not fooling anyone!" I want to shout. "I can totally see you checking your text messages." Some students don't even try to hide it—the phone is right there on the desk, where a pen or highlighter would have

EILEEN DOMBO, PhD, MSW, LICSW is an associate professor, assistant dean, and chair of the MSW program at The Catholic University of America's National Catholic School of Social Service. She teaches practice classes in the program's clinical concentration, and her research interests include clinical models of practice; effective therapeutic intervention techniques for social workers in trauma treatment; and the links between trauma work and vicarious trauma. Dr. Dombo is the former clinical director of the DC Rape Crisis Center and she continues to provide trauma treatment through her private practice and consulting work. Dr. Dombo chairs the Child Protection Board for the Archdiocese of Washington. Based on her work and reputation among her peers, she was named a "Top Therapist" by Washingtonian Magazine.
dombo@cua.edu

been in days of old. I understand that many students juggle kids, work, elder care, and other life responsibilities outside of school. I certainly did when I was a student, but I had to learn to put aside the outside world and immerse myself in what was happening in the classroom if I was going to learn to be attuned to my clients. Of course, life encroached at times, like when my boss paged me (remember beepers?) while I was in the middle of a final exam, and I had to excuse myself to respond to this "urgent" request for my attention, actually not an emergency at all. Attunement must be practiced, like building a muscle. Over time, you are able to pay close attention for longer periods of time, but it is difficult when first starting out. It is similar to getting comfortable sitting with silence and not having to fill the time and space with words. The longer I have practiced, the more comfortable I have become with silence, the more I am able to push aside my own thoughts and concerns and attend to the world of my client. When distractions are so much more prevalent due to the buzzing of the phone or the pop-up windows in our computer screen, does that make it harder for us to stay focused?

In my experience, most students use technology for learning purposes in the classroom, but those who are not can be a distraction to others. Students have let me know that a peer's non-academic use of their laptop was distracting. I've walked around the class while lecturing to find students who had multiple windows open on their desktop, one of which was the PowerPoint document for the lecture, while the others were for on-line shopping, social media, and other unrelated pursuits. I've had to ban the use of technology in the classroom for a small handful of students who just can't handle the privilege. Many others walk the thin line between appropriate and inappropriate use. This is not just a "kids today" complaint shared while ancient ivory-tower professors in dusty academic robes roll their eyes. Older students returning to school for a second or third career are just as susceptible to the lure of the screen. Heck, even I pull out my phone in a less-than-engaging lecture at a conference or during a faculty meeting that drones on a bit too long. Words with Friends awaits. Plus, I've just figured out this whole Pinterest thing, which is pretty fun. While I know that there may be more fascinating things to turn one's attention to than my lecture on working with survivors of sexual trauma, what concerns me is that this work requires attunement. Therapy requires the clinician to pay close attention, notice even the slightest non-verbal cue, and track both content and process with our clients. How can we possibly practice this in the classroom when technological distractions abound?

I've noticed a similar issue with technology in sessions with clients. A parallel process perhaps? I've sat with couples where one turns their attention to their phone screen when their partner is saying something they don't want to hear. Clients have answered their phone during session, read entire strings of text messages to me to add context to relational problems, and more. I get to see photos of loved ones I might not otherwise see. While this is all grist for the mill, it leaves me wondering what impact this will have on professional relationships between clients and therapists. If it is difficult for us to stay focused on our clients, is it, in turn, difficult for them to connect with us? If our clients are distracted in session by their phones, do we become less engaged? I ask clients about the presence of their phones in session. Sometimes the phone feels like another person. This can be helpful, providing more context to the situations they are distressed by, while other times the distraction of the device interrupts deep work. Maybe that's intentional, maybe not.

I wondered what is happening with students now in training. I supervised over 50 trainees from the mid-1990s to the mid-2000s at a small nonprofit agency providing therapy to sexual trauma survivors. I contacted Tammi, who is the clinical director and in charge of the clinical student trainees. I had the pleasure of teaching Tammi from 2010-2012, and now she holds the job I held 12 years ago. I did not have these concerns then; does she have them now? I asked Tammi if she has noticed any difficulties students have with being attuned to their clients, and if she thinks the presence of phones and other devices in the learning environment has anything to do with that. Immediately, she responded with experiences that resonated with this issue. She said it has been a concern of hers in the past few years, stating that it shows up as early as the first two weeks of student training sessions. She notices that students use their phones as a self-soothing tool; during the trainings, when topics get intense, the screens come out. The training days are long, and she finds that the trainees can't sustain attention beyond an hour and a half. She is concerned about the trainees' ability to tolerate the distress caused by the material while with clients, when they can't reach for a device to distract and soothe.

Tammi has had to talk to some students about their level of engagement in the trainings and in staff meetings. They are surprised to hear that it leaves a bad professional impression to scroll through their phone during staff meeting instead of appearing to be connected and engaged with the topics at hand. They often demonstrate a lack of ability to tune in and show they care. She uses supervision to discuss how this may be playing out in group and individual therapy sessions. Tammi reports that she sees a lack of awareness of how using technology can appear unprofessional, and concerns about attunement in sessions are "not even on their radar." Interestingly, Tammi's students will tell her that their clients will show them photos on their phones, and they don't know how to respond; that it feels like a boundary violation that is "too personal." The parallel process implications are interesting. The phone feels very intimate, and they are not quite sure what to do with that. Tammi has also noticed that students are struggling with retaining information from the trainings once they get into the work. Since they aren't tuned in, they miss important information which they then ask her for later. Short attention spans and lack of ability to not be distracted by technology are not a good combination for therapists. Tammi has noticed a level of impatience with talk therapy and wonders if this is linked to shorter attention spans or inability to self-soothe with their phone when they get activated. She worries that current trainees are not learning important ways to self-soothe, and that this will have negative impacts on them and their clients. What will this mean for the 50-minute individual therapy hour or the 90-minute group session?

The importance of being attuned as a therapist was born with the work of attachment theorist John Bowlby and built upon by numerous others, including Dan Siegel (Wylie & Turner, 2011). To connect with clients and create a reparative experience, therapists must attend to verbal and non-verbal cues to sense and interpret communications so that our clients feel understood by us, and in turn understand themselves and their experiences. Is our brain's ability to regulate affect stunted by technology? Do mirror neurons fire in FaceTime? If most of our conversations happen over text messages, do we feel emotionally connected? Siegel argues that relationships shape brain development through "interpersonal neurobiology" (2012, p. 3). The therapist's attunement has to be conveyed through such fine-tuned expressions as tone of voice, eye contact, facial expressions, and the way one holds one's body. How can we stay present when we feel compelled to look at a screen instead of hold a gaze? Research in this area is crucial not only for therapy and education of future therapists, but for all human relatedness.

References
Siegel, D. (2012). *The developing mind: How relationships and the brain interact to shape who we are (2nd ed)*. New York: Guildford Press.

Wylie, M. S., & Turner, L. T. (2011). The attuned therapist: Does attachment theory really matter? *The Psychotherapy Networker, 35*(2).

> It has become appallingly obvious that our technology has exceeded our humanity.
> —Albert Einstein

The Ego at Sunset
Blake Edwards

Having lost all will

to be the man at early morning

considering powers and truth and beauty

Automaton of posts,

comments, likes, statuses, tags, and tweets

that reboot the schizoid with a social platform

A spiritual void

lays the groundwork for the

brilliant, manipulative greed

No longer

to acquire property or profit

but marketing ourselves for attention

Identity becomes property

and the risk of irrelevance or nonexistence

contingent on the degree of their chance clicks.

Leyla Mahbod Kenny

Leyla Mahbod Kenny, PhD, LICSW, has been a psychotherapist in the Washington, DC, area for 18 years. She is faculty at the Washington School of Psychiatry and adjunct faculty at Catholic University, where she is known for her genuine and authentic teaching style. In addition, Leyla has been teaching yoga and mindfulness in the Washington area for 20 years. She has complex feelings towards technology—a love/hate relationship! Leyla@washingtondcpsychotherapy.com

Todd Essig's Conference on Technology and Intimacy

In the *Voices* Spring 1979 issue, author Irma Lee Shepherd wrote an article titled "Intimacy in Psychotherapy." Shepherd states, "...many of the problems which bring people to seek psychotherapy ... have to do with failure to achieve closeness with others, fear of intimacy, lack of skill in making contact, or knowing how to support or maintain satisfying relationships" (p. 9). In my practice and in my own psychotherapy, I have witnessed the same universal longing—a desire to be emotionally intimate with our feelings and to share these feelings in a secure relationship with another.

On February 24, 2018, the Washington School of Psychiatry, in Washington, DC, hosted Todd Essig, PhD, who presented a conference titled "Reclaiming Intimacy: Helping Couples and Couple Therapists Deal with Technology's Influence on Sex, Tenderness, and Closeness." At the conference, we took a deep look at how intimacy is affected by advances in technology. In particular, Essig helped clinicians build awareness of how technology use influences our ability to be emotionally intimate with our clients.

In this article, I will summarize the conference and offer some personal and clinical perspectives. You will also find the transcript of a short interview I conducted with Dr. Essig by phone.

Conference Summary

Dr. Essig's presentation focused on how technology is reshaping intimacy not just between couples but in all relationships including with family, friends, sexual partners, and therapists. Throughout, he directed attention to the way technology use always involves both gains and losses.

History of Technology with the Telegraph

Essig took us on a historical journey to the first uses of technology for connection over distance—the telegraph. The telegraph has been called the Victorian Internet (Standage, 1998). For the first time in human history, one could communicate across distance in real time. Essig shared with us a love story from an 1879 novel titled *Wired Love: A Romance of Dots and Dashes* by Ella Cheever Thayer. In this novel, a couple develops a love for each other first through the telegraph as operators, but then they struggle with their real-life body-to-body relationship.

Definitions

Essig defined the following terms:
- **Screen Relations.** Technologically-mediated simulations of traditional physically co-present relationship experiences based on the experience of telepresence.
- **Telepresence.** Telepresence is the illusion of non-mediation when participating in technologically-mediated relating (see https://ispr.info/about-presence-2/about-presence/ for comprehensive discussion). It provides the feeling of being *there* when *here*, of being with someone when you are sitting alone. Telephones facilitate telepresence by making a faraway voice feel close. As was illustrated in a video of people using smartphones and bumping into things, if you are telepresent elsewhere then you are not present where you are—for instance if you text while driving—then the actuality of where you are will eventually demand your presence. Much time was spent on how telepresence limits the richness of experience because the risks and consequences of being bodies together are fundamentally changed.

Todd Essig

Todd Essig is a training and supervising analyst at the William Alanson White Institute in New York City. He is a well-regarded expert in the field of technology-mediated therapy and relationships. He writes "Managing Mental Wealth" for *Forbes*, where he covers the intersection of technology, public life and private experience. He maintains a busy clinical practice where he treats individuals and couples.

Three Dimensions of Difference with Screen Relations

- **Risks.** We learn to trust the world by taking risks. Being in the Daytona 500 is obviously filled with much more risk than playing a racing video game. If you eliminate the possibility of being dropped, you also eliminate the possibility of being held. This statement stood out to me because I see it played out in my clinical work. I work hard to create a nurturing safe space for my clients to be held so they can be emotionally vulnerable and intimate in our therapeutic relationship. If my clients feel held, then they will be more willing to let me witness the full expression of their feelings and being. If they fear being dropped, then I can witness their anxiety and resistance in the therapeutic relationship. In addition, being bodies together risks experiencing rage, eroticism, and passion in the presence of the body eliciting those feelings. One can act on those feelings. Screen relations do not afford these risks. As psychotherapists, we want the therapeutic experience to pose these risks so we can understand our clients' defenses. If my client is experiencing rage towards me, then I want to see how their psyche navigates their rage in the room with me. We can learn more about the client's processing and make tweaks to align with the client's goals. At the same time, as the therapist, when being bodies together, I can experience a full range of emotions towards my client, which helps me learn more about possible projections, transference, and countertransference reactions.
- **Repleteness or richness of screen relations.** Direct body experience is replete with infinite possi-

bility. Screen relations limit the depth of experience by shrinking our shared experience. At times when my clients have been out of town, I have conducted teletherapy and our shared space is limited to a small screen. The teletherapy sessions serve as a bridge for times when my clients are away. However, I believe our shared experience in these sessions is limited—we miss the physical intimacy of being in the same space, and as a result, the depth of emotional intimacy can be at risk. Yet, I have noticed in a few teletherapy sessions my clients have let themselves be more emotionally vulnerable than is usual when we are being bodies together in one office. Perhaps they feel less vulnerable behind the screen and it seems safer to let down their defenses.

- **Relational Processing.** We evolved to be social creatures. Neuroscientists are starting to uncover the different processing that occurs in the brain when one engages in a screen relationship versus a body-to-body relationship. My colleagues and friends often tell me that I can be extremely focused and that I have a strong memory. Yet I find myself expending energy to focus and struggle to remember transitions and details in my teletherapy sessions. Essig shared that providers of remote treatment frequently report similar experiences. I am sure I am engaging different parts of my brain and my body when I see clients in my office as opposed to on the screen.

Screen Relations with Family and Friends

Technology allows constant connection but with less intimacy. It can be difficult to be intimate with family and friends, and as a result people turn to the screens for comfort. Ironically, screens are becoming the solution to interpersonal discomfort created by spending too much time on screens. When we find ourselves using screens in the presence of others, then we are *almost present* and not giving or receiving undivided attention.

Essig cited a research study conducted by Highlights magazine (2014) on the "state of the kid": 62% of the children interviewed described their parents as too distracted to listen. When asked what distracted their parents, 51% said technology.

Screen Relations and Romance

Essig described various aspects of technology and romance. He looked at how technology influences sexual development, sexting, hook-up culture, online dating, and Internet porn.

Technology provides both positive and negative results for a person going through sexual development. The Internet can offer validation and information. On the flipside, there is a peril in comparing oneself to others who seem prettier, sexier, and/or more experienced. The pornification of sexual knowledge affects people's sexual expectations. Finally, the Internet can be a platform for sexual bullying.

Sexting is increasingly common among adolescents and adults. Young people risk emotional harm and legal risk from sexting. As we know through media, adults can also face professional consequences.

Fear of missing out (FOMO) and the conveniences afforded by technology have resulted in a strong hook-up culture. Devices make it easier to simultaneously seek sexual intimacy and hide from it. Texting makes the negotiation to hook up easy. People who are depressed tend to feel better when they hook up. People who feel good tend to feel worse after hooking up.

Romance has certainly been affected by the option to pursue online dating. Dating sites are not efficient dating marketplaces despite advertising themselves that way. The sites are designed to be "sticky" by getting people to continually come back to the site.

People are also not necessarily going online to find a mate, which also results in people staying on these sites. Why do people pursue online dating?

Examples of complex motivation to pursue online dating:

- **Always someone better:** Online dating affords the possibility to find someone better.
- **Ambivalence:** People can shop around and soothe their FOMO.
- **Act as another person:** Some people pretend to be someone else online to get responses without actually meeting the other people.
- **Putting a toe in the water:** Some may flirt online but do not follow up with meeting others.

Internet Porn accounts for 30% of all Internet traffic. Essig described some of the immense advances in porn technology. For example, cam-girls and cam-boys are real people who offer personal conversations through the Internet. Teledildonics are Bluetooth-enabled sex toys with synchronized feedback to the cam-girl or cam-boy. The viewer can control the sex toy which the cam-girl or cam-boy uses. Porn is driving an immense amount of the tech world's inventions in virtual reality.

Porn addiction is a not an actual addiction. People do experience problems with overuse. Essig warns that use of the addiction model explains away something new with an older model just to make it seem more understandable. New models are needed. He suggested that over-use is simulation entrapment (opposite of simulation avoidance) run amok. With simulation entrapment, one loses awareness of the fact that it is a simulation and thinks the simulation is a reality. People respond to the emotional illusion of telepresence.

Screen Relations in Clinical Practice

How is technology changing the face of therapy? A few years ago at an ethics conference, I met a colleague who worked for an agency which provides teletherapy. I asked her, "What would a clinician do if their client is suicidal and needs immediate care?" She said the agency collects a list of emergency numbers and suicide hotlines for the client's area. I remember also asking about malpractice and licensing issues related to teletherapy. Does a clinician need to be licensed in both the state where they practice from and where the client lives? Or does the clinician only need to be licensed in the state where they sit with their screen? Do laws on teletherapy vary state by state? *(See "The Ten Tech Commandments" in this issue.)*

We need to be aware of both gains and losses of teletherapy and not focus on one being good or bad. Teletherapy can help serve as a bridge when our clients are traveling or perhaps help clients living in remote areas (with Internet). I know in various American Indian reservations, tribes have limited access to health care professionals including dentists, specialists, and mental health workers. We must also be conscious of technology cons which include: a lack of a holding environment, continuous partial attention, and difficulty with silence (during the silence we may be wondering if the technology is not working). It is important that the better-than-nothing does not slide over into being routinely accepted as good-enough practice.

Could therapists eventually be replaced by artificial intelligence (AI)? Some programs and apps are expected to replace real-life therapists. Essig showed us a program with an algorithm to provide an avatar (a computer-generated representation) of a therapist. The avatar read both verbal and non-verbal communication from the client and then provided real-time interventions. I was shocked because the avatar provided many of the same interventions I would have used! But what about the unconscious communication I experience with my clients? There is no way an algorithm can pick up on unconscious dialogue. As clinicians, we must continue to build our conscious awareness on the benefits of being bodies together—these benefits (safe holding environment, in-person focus, the opportunity to be held and dropped, unconscious therapeutic alliance, etc.) are hard to simulate with AI. Technology allows intimacy to develop but technology has limits, uses different processes, and can involve unintended consequences.

Four Take-Aways from the Conference

After attending the conference and speaking directly with Todd Essig, I have the following four take-aways:

1. **"Technology is not a luxury, it is a necessity."** Barack Obama shared this quote at the 2015 ConnectHome announcement in Oklahoma, which promoted Internet connection to everyone including remote tribal nations. Technology is here, and we must adjust to it. Many of our clients use technology daily and we must have an experiential working knowledge of technology to relate to them. Personally, I am someone who lives techno-light: I rarely watch TV, keep all electronics (except my battery powered alarm clock) out of my bedroom, and do not have a personal Facebook or Twitter account. However, I do use technology to help me with my private practice: I have a website with forms and policies for my clients; I schedule appointments through email; I accept credit card payments on my smartphone; and my clients text or call me when they are running late for appointments. If I had a repulsive stance towards technology, I would be doing my practice and clients a disservice.
2. **Take a broad liberal arts perspective.** Look at technology from multiple angles to find the pros and cons. For my undergraduate studies, I attended Dickinson College, a small liberal arts college where I focused on political philosophy. I loved these courses because we were never trying to find a truth but rather contemplated various philosophies. In a similar light, technology provides us with a new way of being, and we can find both the pros and cons in this. By embracing some technology, I am not turning a blind eye to its limits. Rather, I am trying to stay alert to the perils while also taking advantage of the gains.
3. **Use the screen as a window to build self-awareness.** The screen can be a window to help us learn what our clients want to see and also to help us deepen our understanding of who our clients are. Sometimes, my clients want to share certain pictures from their smartphones with me—a picture of a deceased loved one, a fiancé, their child, etc. I always accept their offer. My clients physically come closer to me when they share this picture from their device. At this point, my anxiety goes up. However, despite my anxiety about my personal space, the experience seems extremely rich. In these moments, my clients are showing me what they want me to see. I can then relate this back and help them build more self-awareness about what is important to them.
4. **In-person learning and connection have substance but screen relations can serve as a bridge when there is no road.** As I mentioned earlier, I prefer to meet with my clients in person. However, if my clients go out of town, I would rather keep the momentum of our work with the option of teletherapy as a bridge between our in-person sessions.

Interview with Dr. Todd Essig

Leyla Kenny: There is a joke about a man asking his wife to pull the plug if he were ever brain dead. The wife then gets up and pulls the plug on the TV. As we've seen over the years, many couples have a difference in how they view their use of technology. How do you help couples (or individuals in treatment who are part of a couple) negotiate their different styles of technology use?

Todd Essig: You deal with it like anything else. Use whatever your style clinically is in dealing with conflicts with a couple. But adding an active consideration of your own conflicts with technology use can be helpful. Clinicians need to be aware of their own conflicts and influences with technology. And if their style is to self-disclose about their use of technology in the session, then that's ok. Or if their style is to keep a more neutral stance, that's ok as well.

Kenny: Are there times when porn or sexting would be recommended by a clinician (such as one partner with a higher libido than the other, or someone with a disability)? And if so, how would you prevent simulation entrapment?

Essig: Someone who provides more directive sex therapy would be better to answer that. Most likely a sex therapist does recommend porn and other devices to their clients at times.

Kenny: How does a clinician explore the client's use of porn or sexting while also taking into consideration the moral/ethical issues of porn such as the possible exploitation of young women?

Essig: When I was early in my career working at a public hospital in a disadvantaged area, there was a court referral of someone released from prison who had killed her three kids by chaining them to a radiator when she went on a crack binge. She had no remorse. I could not work with this woman. I can work with some clients who do some things that are unethical and illegal, but not all. Clinicians need to go through their own moral reckoning to be as helpful as we can to people who come through our offices in distress. If a clinician has their own moral conflict with pornography and is unable to help the patient because of that conflict, then they need to refer to someone else. We need to help the person in distress if we can rather than impose our moral framework.

Kenny: As you mention, we can all become aware of both the gains and losses of screen relations. As a clinician, do you personally see more gains or more losses?

Essig: The way to manage the inevitably of gains and losses is to develop self-awareness, because without that there is overwhelming loss. The pathology of screen relations has avoidance and entrapment. But we need to see all that technology affords without losing sight of the loss. We need to be fully aware of what we are doing in the moment and see how technology use is changing who we are and how we relate to people.

References

Highlights (2014). Retrieved from: https://www.highlights.com/sites/default/files/public/sotk2014.pdf

Shepherd, I. (1979). Intimacy in psychotherapy. *Voices: The Art and Science of Psychotherapy, 15*(1), pp. 9-12.

Thayer, E.C. (1879). *Wired love: A romance of dots and dashes.* New York: W.J. Johnston, Publisher.

Michael Giordano

Sex and Love in the Digital Age

Woof! Nice looking man there!
Thanks! Good looking man yourself.
Glad you think so. I'm Mike.
Hi, Mike. I'm Dan.

BASED IN WASHINGTON, DC, MICHAEL GIORDANO has been a clinical social worker since 1999. He earned his MSW from the University of Maryland, Baltimore, and worked in small nonprofits before entering private practice in 2007. While serving a wide range of clients and their concerns, his main interests are gender identity, trauma, and sex therapy. Mike is also a dad and an avid yogi.
www.WhatIHearYouSaying.com
Mike.Giordano.MSW@gmail.com

SO BEGAN A CHAT BETWEEN ME AND "DAN" ON SCRUFF, A MOBILE DATING AND HOOK-UP APP FOR GAY, QUEER, AND BI MEN. This app is GPS-based, meaning the profiles, or pictures of men, are arranged based on their distance from you. It looks like the "Hollywood Squares" layout—a grid of pictures right there on your phone screen. Some men have a picture of their face, others a picture of their pecs. A few are either blank or have a random picture of a landscape or, if they're feeling playful, a rooster. Men are on Scruff and similar apps (Grindr, Jack'd, Recon, and such) for many reasons. Some are "looking for" sex. ("What are you looking for?" is a common question on these apps.) Others are looking for friends. Some are looking for dates. And many are looking for a combination of these "relationships." Dan appears to be open to hookups, friends, and dating; as I am.

Dan's pic is his face and upper body, his upper body is actually clothed, which is often not the case. I find Dan incredibly handsome. And his profile, the part where individuals can describe themselves, is interesting too. He seems to be just my type. I am very happy that he appears to be interested in me.

We flirt a bit. We share more pictures of ourselves. We discuss mutual interests, how long we've each been in the city and why we came here. We might even discuss a little bit about our sexual interests to see if we match. Dan asks what I do for a living. I tell Dan that I'm a psychotherapist. He tells me his profession. And we chat about our careers for a bit. Then he tells me something I did not at all expect. *I think you were my ex's therapist. And I know he talked about me with you.*

I immediately feel some disappointment. I start bargaining with myself about whether I can continue chatting with Dan. I text a friend of mine who's also a therapist and has been in similar situations when he had an online dating life. After talking with him, my next move becomes clear. I reluctantly tell Dan that I can't continue with the chat.

This is just one of many incidents where my professional and personal lives converge in the virtual world. While Washington, DC, is a major metropolitan area, the gay community, compared to the straight community, is fairly small. For example, there are maybe seven gay bars in DC, compared to an untold number of mainstream or straight bars. It's not at all unusual to see familiar faces in predominantly gay spaces. And it's even more insular if you have volunteered or worked in LGBTQ organizations, which I have done many times. For many gay and queer men in this town, six degrees of separation is extreme. There might be one or two degrees in most cases. On Facebook, it's unusual for me to not have a "mutual friend" with another gay man in this city.

To make matters more complicated, I also see lots of gay and queer men in my private practice. And due to the size of the gay community, it often seems I can't go to a gay bar without seeing a current or former client. In fact, last year, I was at an event in Chicago and there were a couple of former clients in attendance as well. It makes sense that I would have a similar experience online.

About seven years ago, all of this was new to me. I had ended a 17-year, monogamous relationship. I had had little experience dating or hooking up—and certainly none with mobile applications. Additionally, I received no professional training about navigating these potential conflicts as a therapist. But I was curious. I wanted to date. And I wanted to have sexual experiences. Apps such as Grindr and Scruff were popular, and I was intrigued. I was also hesitant. The first question I had to address was if it was appropriate and ethical for me, a therapist, to have a presence in this medium.

Good boundaries are clearly important to maintain as a therapist, and disclosure is something we assess before initiating. We want to make sure that what we tell clients about ourselves is in their best interest. While there are many perspectives on the level of disclosure that should occur in the consulting room, there is rarely a discussion of how we should navigate the virtual world. Some therapists very much limit their online presence, refusing to have a Facebook page, much less a Match.com profile. For me, as a single man, I found this approach too limiting. I did not want to become resentful of my profession. And I wanted to meet men. It seemed to me that being a good therapist and being on dating and hook-up apps did not have to be mutually exclusive. I also did not want to hurt my professional standing with clients. Seeing their therapist on a dating or hook-up app could be jarring, provoke judgment, or stir up sexual thoughts about me, especially if there was already an attraction. It would be naive to think this couldn't have a negative impact on the relationship.

To confront this dilemma, I did two things. First, I spoke with other gay male therapists about their decisions regarding being on the apps; I listened to how they considered their relationships to themselves as sexual people as well as how they work with clients. Additionally, I spent several sessions with my therapist/supervisor, Jonathan, exploring boundaries and relationships. Jonathan and I began our dive into this topic when

I first became single. I knew I wanted to be online. I wanted to experience this aspect of gay life and I wanted to meet more people in general. But I was concerned about what people would think of me. Would clients find it unsavory? Would I be judged by my colleagues? Would I judge myself if I struggled with some internalized sex-shaming messages like, "It's slutty to have a profile on such an app"? I experienced a battle within that drew from my upbringing and conditioning, professional ethics, self-worth, and self-realization. Jonathan helped me explore my judgments about what constitutes a proper sexual expression, calling out beliefs that belied my identity as a sex-positive person and therapist. I noticed and challenged the shame and embarrassment I felt when talking about my desires, explored my varied reactions when I saw people I knew on the apps, and used this information to help me be more open to myself. Of course, as I became more accepting of my own sexual desires and expressions, I was able to do the same for my clients, growing more comfortable talking with them about their activity on the apps and how they internalized it. I also knew I needed to be prepared to talk with clients about my presence on the apps. And I had enough conversations with other therapists, particularly gay male therapists, about how they navigate the cyber world with their clients to decide that I could do this as well.

There were several options of mobile gay dating and hook-up apps in which to enroll. I decided to go with Scruff as it had a wider diversity of men I found attractive. I then had to figure out how I would present myself. With several decisions to make, I asked my gay male therapist friends about their decision-making processes. Would I use a face picture in my profile or have a picture that was more anonymous? An anonymous profile would allow me to give more personal, and perhaps sexual, information about myself. But I would also need to screen other anonymous profiles more assertively. To make sure I was not communicating with a client, I would need to require them to share a face pic with me before I sent mine. If I chose to post a public picture of myself, would I be shirtless? How would I describe myself—specifically, would I have anything sexual in my profile? Clients would surely come across my profile, so what was I comfortable with them knowing about me? I decided on a face pic, clothed, with very limited information about my sexual likes and dislikes. I've become comfortable with clients knowing I'm on the apps, but I do think there are things they don't need to know about me, including my HIV status and what sexual positions I prefer. I also gave information about myself that I would feel comfortable with anyone, including clients, knowing, such as hobbies and general interests.

When clients discuss being on the dating and hook-up apps, I've made it a practice to tell them that they may come across my profile, if they haven't already. We spend some time exploring what comes up for them with this information. Clients have told me that these conversations have helped them be even more open about themselves and their desires, somehow loosening up from the shame that often inhibits people from talking about their own sexuality. This recently came up with a client, a middle-aged gay man who has felt sexually repressed most of his life. He was not on any apps but was very curious. Alongside his curiosity was also shame, emanating from a Catholic upbringing as well as the mainstream culture, which has told him for years that gay desire is sinful and disgusting, and should be hidden. Within this discussion, I informed him that he would likely come across my profile, asking how he imagines he would feel seeing me there. He told me that knowing I was online somehow "gave him permission" to do the same, feeling less guilt about doing something "wrong."

Another practice is to "block" clients when I come across their profiles. Blocking makes it so neither of us can see the other's profile. It is a way of creating some space in the virtual world, while I still inhabit it. I'm glad this option exists as well.

I have more stories about my virtual professional lives colliding. There was the time that a former client came up to me at a bar asking, very flirtatious and probably a bit drunk, why I was "playing with him" on Grindr. I had no idea what he was talking about as I never flirt with clients—current or former. He said he'd sent me anonymous messages from a profile without a face pic, flirting with me, and I never responded. At first, I was taken aback, especially when he grabbed me by the shirt. I said I hadn't known it was him messaging me and that I don't talk with clients, current or former, on the apps. I tried to be firm, non-shaming, and brief. It was an awkward encounter, to say the least, but I was proud of myself for how I engaged in it.

There was also the time I was going to meet a man who was in an open relationship with another couple for coffee. The evening before the coffee date, it became clear to me that he was in a relationship with a couple I was currently working with in therapy. I immediately needed to find a way to ethically get out of the date without breaking confidentiality. In a message, I told him that I could not meet up with him. He asked why, so I responded, "I'm a psychotherapist." He immediately responded, "Are you Dr. Mike?" and began to tell me that his partners were seeing me. I did not confirm that with him, but when his partners, my clients, came in for their session later that week, I informed them of the interaction. They were not surprised, stating that their partner had told them. We discussed this for a bit longer and I continued to work with the couple successfully for months to come.

To navigate the online dating world, a therapist needs to embody a willingness to have difficult conversations with clients and to have clients see you as a sexual person. What I inherently understood, but now has now become explicit, is that clients can already see me as a sexual being, and I am fooling myself if I think that there is an impervious boundary between my personal and professional worlds. I now pay more attention and address it when a client seems to flirt with me in session, rather than dismiss it or hope I misunderstood, as I used to. Those conversations have led to deeper work with clients, utilizing our relationship to help them understand themselves better. And I still get to live my life authentically as much as my clients work to live theirs. ▼

Life as a Text-Based Therapist

Erika Bugaj

Early on in my career as an online, text-based therapist, I mistakenly voice-recorded myself picking my kids up from school as my first message to a new client. I am sure it was just a lot of banal noises and maybe some silly baby talk as I put the kids in the car to go home. The next message I left was a sincere apology for my first impression with this new client. It was met with understanding. Mostly, that has been my experience of my online, text-based clients: they understand that life is unpredictable, messy and busy. Maybe that is why they choose text over showing up in my office.

Recently, a client voice-recorded some after-dinner conversations between herself and some friends. Again, it was a mistake (I think) and this time it was hers. Is it significant? Maybe, maybe not. As Irvin Yalom says in his book *The Gift of Therapy* (2002), "It's all grist for the mill."

And so it has been going on two years of online, mostly text-based therapy with some video sessions interspersed throughout.

I was encouraged by a therapist colleague to give this online text-based therapy platform a try. It was a whim and felt more like a hobby at first, a complement to my face-to-face therapy practice. Perhaps a second income stream to support my growing family. I wrote to my clients in the mornings with coffee and again as I nursed my young son to sleep at night. It became as routine as brushing my teeth.

At first I struggled to turn words as I would speak them in individual therapy sessions into text-based messages. How do you communicate to clients you've never seen or spoken to the empathy, validation, understanding, and felt human experience that conveys when you sit and look into their eyes? How would I authentically acknowledge their existence, struggles, challenges and vulnerability?

I felt it should come naturally to me, as a lifelong journal- and letter-writer. I always enjoyed writing letters and putting them in the mail. I had long-term correspondences with my grandmothers, friends, and some childhood pen pals. Once email became accessible in my early college years, my best friend and I kept up that way writing detailed notes about our lives. However, texting did not come naturally, and soon I had one of the seasoned text-based therapists coaching me.

Erika Bugaj, MA, MSW, LICSW, is a practicing psychotherapist with specialties in working with children, adolescents, college-age students, families, expectant parents, and in perinatal mood and anxiety disorders. A former elementary school teacher, Erika has also completed postgraduate study in psychodynamic psychotherapy with children and adolescents. Erika enjoys the arts and sometimes incorporates artwork and creativity into her clinical work. She is founder and director of Dandelion Psychotherapy, PLLC, serving families in Washington, DC. She is also a therapist on the Talkspace online therapy platform. Erika resides in Washington, DC, with her two children and rescue dog.
erika.l.bugaj@gmail.com

Once I practiced for a while, I got the hang of it. I have to turn words and non-verbal gestures—the reflections, empathetic nod, and eye contact—into text-based missives to help them wade through grief and loss, dismantle anxiety, and swim to the surface of their depression. Most of my entries end with a question for reflection.

How have I done it time-wise and otherwise? Many ask me. Over the course of my online therapy career, I've raised two small children, run my in-person psychotherapy practice, separated from my husband and then divorced.

I shudder to think of the reactions of some colleagues I consider "old school psychoanalytic," and how they may resist the shift from face-to-face sessions to anything written via text message or streamed online. Oh, the risks! The liabilities! The lack of regulation! The uncertainty of it all.

People come to online therapy for lots of reasons. Clients come to untangle themselves from relationships that have gone wrong. They have lost or are losing themselves. They come to online therapy to sort themselves out. They realize who they were and what parts of themselves they have lost. They come for rediscovery. They look for changes they can make in others and then realize one of my mantras, "We cannot change others—we can only change ourselves." It is not easy to accept. With some face-to-face clients, I verbally repeat this many times. With my online clients, I just type it many times, in different ways. Eventually they get it, and maybe they leave, just like I did. I love it when I get to witness them starting over in new healthier relationships. Those who have inspire hope in me that I will someday have the same.

It has been rewarding to work with clients who remain clients for a long time—months, even years. Some build trust slowly. One client, after 18 months, just sent me a photo of herself for the first time. Some I never see on video chat or speak to live. I never have seen their faces or heard their voices. They are just putting words on my iPhone screen, words that have caused me to get a prescription for bifocals at the ripe old age of 41.

In the mornings, I write from the couch with coffee. In the evenings, now that my son is weaned, I sometimes let my kids read their Kindles in bed with me while I write to clients. Sometimes they have already gone to sleep, and I slip out to the front porch and type or listen to clients' messages. Now I might peruse messages while I quickly walk my newly-adopted dog. I wonder if my clients are nearby in a neighborhood close to me, cooking their dinner, or tucked into bed in a far-away corner of the city. Sometimes I wonder if I rub elbows with them at happy hour or the grocery store. I don't look much like my professional photo anymore. I've changed my hair color a bit and cut it. I have new glasses. Would they recognize their online therapist? Even if so, I might not know who they are. There is some comfort in anonymity for us both.

Recently I began to self-disclose a bit more. Some of my clients know I'm recently divorced, I'm a single mom, what neighborhood I reside in, a little about my kids, and adventures I've had with my dog. I find it brings us closer, sharing the common threads that hold us together. As SARK, one of my favorite authors, writes, "We are all swimming in the soup together." ▼

References

SARK. (2000). *Transformation soup: Healing for the splendidly imperfect.* New York: Fireside.
Yalom, I. (2002). *The gift of therapy.* New York: Perennial Library.

Anonymous

A Balancing Act

What happens when a psychotherapist has two identities, one with clients, and one with a live audience on stage? How can these two identities co-exist in the age of social media? What is the conventional wisdom of our profession, and how might it differ from one's values and lived experience? How does one balance personal and professional selves? I've given a lot of thought to each of these questions and believe that my story might be of use to other therapists dealing with these same issues.

In my Muggle life—my non-magical, mundane life for all you non-Harry Potter fans out there—I'm a therapist primarily for lesbian, gay, bisexual, transgender, queer, intersex, asexual, ethically non-monogamous, kinky, and sex worker folk. In my superhero life I'm a burlesque performer. Burlesque is a dance form that became wildly popular in 1920s America after Vaudeville. It accentuates the beauty of the human form through vaudevillian techniques of story-telling and striptease. Both types of work—psychotherapy and burlesque—nourish me in ways that I truly appreciate, but the mix of the two has also caused discomfort in others. The discomfort seems tied to the outdated idea of a psychotherapist serving as a blank slate to clients and the shame others still associate with sex. As a performer I've become adept at marketing and self-promotion through social media, and I've met people in communities that my psychotherapist peers rarely do. These are all experiences that I have built my current practice around. As a therapist, I've learned to keep my superhero identity a secret and separate from my Muggle life. Because of this double life, and potential judgment by other therapists, I have chosen to remain anonymous in this journal.

Performing has been a love of mine from an early age—first theater, then belly dancing, and about a year before enrolling in grad school for psychology, burlesque. At the beginning of graduate school, I wanted to work within the court system or for the FBI. As I finished my first year of school I began to also consider how one's sexual identity intersects with psychology. During my second year of graduate school I told my advisor about my superhero life and she insisted that I quit performing if I wanted to continue in this profession. She didn't feel it was appropriate for someone who wanted to be a psychotherapist to also perform on stage, but I believe her response was related to the type of dance that I performed. Had I been a ballerina I suspect her reaction would not have been as strong. This rubbed me wrong in many ways. I had been performing longer then I had been interested in psychology and I continue to feel there is nothing shameful about being a burlesque performer. Our society has a very puritanical view of nudity and how we interact with it. There is nothing shameful about the human form and sexuality, but we do treat it that way. To most it's something to be used only in procreation, or when it's the female form, to sell someone's product. Burlesque is about empowerment and acceptance of who one is. I felt, if not in any other profession, psychology should have support, compassion, and understanding for someone being their most authentic healthy self. I had even learned of a therapeutic center in my area using burlesque to help individuals manage their anxiety and gain more self-confidence, which I thought was awesome. Through performing I'd met quiet a few folks who identified as kinky, sex workers, or ethically non-monogamous who were also looking for good psychotherapists who could understand and not pathologize who they were. All of this knowledge was spinning in my head and would influence my professional identity in years to come. I declined to follow her advice and I'm happy that I did.

However, her words did stay with me. While I was in graduate school and not yet providing care to clients, it didn't occur to me to stop advertising performances on my personal Myspace (I know I'm dating myself) or Facebook page. In the beginning, I only had a personal Facebook page (using my legal name), but with time I also created a performer page (using my stage name), and they were both completely open to the public. I'm not even sure if there were other security options on Facebook then. The only safety measure I used at that time was to strictly use my stage name for promotion, when I was performing, or when I was interviewed for articles, TV, or podcasts. Much like Clark Kent's glasses, never mixing my superhero and Muggle names kept my two lives a secret from those who didn't know me personally.

Once I began providing care as a case manager in a community mental health clinic, I realized I needed to make some social media changes to ensure these identities remained separate. The clients I cared for were mentally ill, justice-involved and/or survivors of trauma. Although I felt it was unlikely any of them would be in the audience at one of my shows, many were on Facebook. As a budding mental health professional, I wasn't provided any feedback on how to manage my performer persona or social media presence, so I was making it up as I went along. I knew that I didn't want my personal life and choices to confuse or trigger any of my clients. Many of them lacked a sex-positive education and had loose or non-existent boundaries due to negative experiences in their families of origin. At that point I continued using my performer page only for advertising my performances and became very careful of the content of my posts on my personal

Facebook page.

More changes came when a client did show up to a burlesque show that I also attended. I was only an audience member that night, so I didn't have to manage her seeing me on stage. She recognized me in the audience and asked about me being there. We discussed how we were both there to see friends perform. She told me about her friend, who was a first-time performer I didn't know, and we both wished each other a good evening and went our separate ways. I spoke to the other performers I knew and provided them with my Muggle name for the night and said there was a coworker in the audience and I didn't want to out myself to them. Everyone understood, and the night went off without a problem. At our next session I asked my client about her experience at the show, how often she attended shows like those, and if my being there was a problem. She told me she loved seeing her friend, that she only went because her friend was in the show, and she didn't have any concerns about seeing me out in the world. Our city is pretty small and this client was interested in or part of many of the same communities and activities I was—cosplay, conventions, live performance, kink—and she also identified as bisexual. I felt there was a good chance there would be another overlap down the line, so we reviewed how we would interact in public. At that time, I decided if she or any client did see me on a promotional flyer around the city, I would explain I was a belly dancer—a style of dance I believed was more socially acceptable—and then discuss with them how and why it would be inappropriate for them to attend a show.

In the past few years, I have received quite a bit of feedback and training through ethical continuing education courses. I've consulted with my supervisor—another psychotherapist in the community who provides the type of psychotherapy I do while also belonging to many of the communities they serve—and with a psychotherapist who does not provide psychotherapy to the varied communities and is also not a part of them. Currently I am a solo practitioner in the field and am a member of many of the communities I serve.

As of this moment I have a Muggle Facebook page, a psychotherapy Facebook page, and Twitter, Instagram, and Facebook accounts for my superhero persona. I've been interviewed on podcasts and documentaries, and I have taught classes, as a psychotherapist and as a performer in separate spheres. I am well-respected as a performer, and I am well-respected as a psychotherapist. My marketing skills have propelled both careers forward.

As I mentioned previously, in graduate school I was interested in the idea of how sexual identity and psychotherapy intersect. I have recently started the journey of becoming a certified sex therapist. During sex therapy supervision, my supervisor and I have processed what it means to be a psychotherapist and a performer. My supervisor has known me for some time and has always known about my double life, but questions about my double life had come up from others, who asked me to consult with two other psychotherapists as well. I was worried about what might come out of these ethics consultations. I was overwhelmingly assured by the consulting psychotherapists that there wasn't anything shameful about my performing, and I wasn't causing harm to my clients by having this double life. This took a huge weight off my shoulders. I had assumed they would have the same reaction as my graduate school advisor.

I was given feedback about how I might create clear boundaries between my performing life and my clients. Here are some of those suggestions. First, I was told to not have a personal Facebook page. In this day and age, that felt like too much to give up, because it's how I keep in touch with the vast majority of people in my life. Instead I decided I would further limit how many public posts I made, continue the practice of only posting personal posts to my friends, and use as many Facebook security options as possible to hide myself from non-friends. I have also talked with my clients and requested that if I appear on their social media feeds or dating apps they hide me, as we cannot interact in that way. So far that request has been overwhelmingly accepted without concern or questions. Most often clients have laughed during the conversation and said that's a boundary they would make themselves, even without me requesting it. As I said before, since I am in many of the communities I serve, I've also talked to my friends about the content of what they tag or post about me.

Second, I was given guidance about how to limit the chances of a client being at a performance and how to manage the situation if it were to happen. Since I've been a solo practitioner, one client that I know of has attended one of my performances. The client was a member of the kink and ethically non-monogamous communities I serve. I was not concerned with this individual attending the performance because the communities they are part of are both body- and sex-positive. In addition, I felt they had good boundaries and our psychotherapy work was not related to trauma, sexual identity, or an unmanaged major mental health diagnosis. With other clients I have processed their feelings and asked about any possible concerns with these crossovers. Since my ethical consults, I take more detailed notes about those conversations with clients and make it clear to clients that if at any point they do have concerns, I am open to discussing them. During those instances none of my clients related any concern, and I did not notice any change in our therapeutic relationship as I continued providing care.

A third recommendation was to cease performing in my geographical area. That was a harder suggestion to follow. The number of my performances has decreased overall because of my busy schedule, and I do perform out of the area when I can.

The final recommendation, which I've had the hardest time adjusting to, was outing myself to my clients. This frankly seemed uncomfortable and weird because it didn't feel like an aspect of my life my clients needed to be privy to. I can still hear that graduate school advisor shaming me for my choices, but a number of the communities I serve interact differently with nudity than mainstream Americans. There's nothing shameful or secretive about nudity to members of certain sex-positive communities, and to them it often seems normal. But I have come to terms with this suggestion and have slowly begun outing myself with clients who—because of the communities they are in, their professions, and/or their activities—I think have the most chance of stumbling upon my performance life. I explain that, due to information I have received through clinical supervision, I would like to make them aware of a part of my life that could possibly affect them. I disclose that I am a performer who also produces a show in the area, and if they happen upon one of my shows to please not attend it and request a refund, as it could negatively impact our therapeutic relationship.

I'm pleased to say that so far not a single client has related any concern about me having a performer life outside of psychotherapy. But I also realize there could be instances when a client might not find out until it's too late. In those instances, we have agreed that they will leave the space for the time that I'm performing, and after my performance has ended they can continue to enjoy the event. In these instances, it would be unlikely I would know unless they brought it up at a future session, but when that happens we will process their feelings or concerns as is necessary and I can even provide referrals if needed.

In the process of outing myself, it has become clear that a number of my clients either knew I was a performer before they sought me out or came upon the information through friends, flyers, or the Internet. Those that sought me out because of this information said they felt I would be less judgmental about their concerns, whether or not they were sex-based. Some have also said that it generally made me more approachable or human and therefore less scary. For those who found out later, they related it fit with the concept they already had of me and it didn't cause them any unease. If anything, they thought it was cool. So again, without knowing, being a performer had positively affected my therapeutic life. Not only had it opened me to communities I could serve but it had also brought clients to my office that might not have otherwise found me.

It's not always easy balancing a superhero life with a Muggle one. Having a diverse life has made me not only a better and more interesting person but also a more open and approachable psychotherapist. As technology continues to evolve, I'm sure our ethical standards and practices will eventually catch up. As they do, I hope they keep in mind that the positives of technology do outweigh most of the negatives. In the meantime, I will continue to have frank conversations with clients and monitor my social media privacy settings. After all, it's a balancing act.

New technology is not good or evil in and of itself. It's all about how people choose to use it.

—David Wong

Tech Talk: Cheating Presence or Enhancing it?

LISA KAYS, LICSW, LCSW-C, is a clinical social worker in private practice in Washington, DC, where she works with individuals, couples and groups. Her professional adventures include writing and training therapists in ethics and social media, as well as integrating improv with therapy. Her improv for therapists classes have been featured on NBC4 and in *The Washington Post*. She lives in Washington, DC, with her husband and almost-three-year-old son, who was asking for a "phon-y" far earlier than she expected.
lisa@lisakays.com

In this interview, Lisa Kays talks with AAP members Damon Blank and Loretta Sparks about the increasing amount of technology in our lives and its impact on therapy and relationships. This conversation emerged from a workshop conducted at the 2016 AAP Institute & Conference in Santa Fe titled, "The Tangled Web of Social Media, Technology and Therapy: New Challenges for the Therapy Relationship," and co-led by Marilyn Schwartz and Lisa Kays. During the workshop, much emerged from participants about the role of technology and therapy; Damon and Loretta represented differing views about it. When asked, they were both happy to hold a bi-coastal phone call to talk and share in more depth.

Kays: When I say the word "technology," what's the first word that comes to mind for each of you?

Sparks: "Goodie."

Blank: "Oy vey!"

Kays: How techy are each of you personally? What do you use the most tech-wise?

Blank: I use a smartphone, tablet, and Bluetooth. But I don't do Twitter and all those other kinds of things. I text and email. I think that's the extent of my technology. Oh yeah, I do Facebook.

Kays: Loretta, what about you?

Sparks: I have all things Apple. I have an iPad, a smartphone, a laptop, and a desktop. My newest toy is a Bose portable speaker…it has a Bluetooth connection that's so cool.

Blank: There's one other thing that I do that blows my mind. When my license was coming up for renewal, I said, "Whoa, do I have enough CEUs?" I went online and took some courses, took the test, and got my CEUs online, which was easy.

Sparks: I have done that as well. I am an information freak. So, the computer and Google. Oh my God, Google tells me everything, I speak to it like I speak to a person.

Blank: As I'm listening, I'm thinking, so maybe I'm not so tech averse as I thought I was.

Sparks: You don't sound like it.

Damon Blank

DAMON BLANK, EdM, is a licensed marriage/family therapist and certified Kundalini Yoga instructor, E-200 RYT 200. He has been in private practice in Medfield, Massachusetts, for over 35 years. He utilizes the intersection of psychotherapy and Kundalini Yoga to nurture his clients' communication, growth, and healing.
damonblanklmft@gmail.com

Loretta Sparks

LORETTA SPARKS, LMFT, DCEP, is a fellow and past president of AAP and a diplomate of comprehensive energy psychotherapy. She is unabashedly fascinated by most things technical, particularly aspects that impact our personal and professional lives. She practices in Hermosa Beach, California.
Loretta@selfcarepower.com

Kays: Are you worried that eventually this will replace us therapists, as healers of the mind, that people will just Google, "How do I fix my anxiety?" and nobody is going to need us anymore?

Blank: I think that knowledge is power, and I want as many people to have power as possible. So I want people to say, "Wow, I can't sleep at night, my heart is racing," and find out, "look at this, I might have generalized anxiety disorder." They may get some ideas that might be helpful. But I think ultimately, we, as psychotherapists, are going to be here forever because what heals people is the relationship and the quality of our communication with people, independent of all this information that's available.

Sparks: I absolutely agree. Knowledge is the gateway to making real adjustments and changes in your life. The problem is, so many of them know what they need to do. They just don't want to pay the emotional price for doing it. It takes another human being bearing witness. There's no machine that can bear witness.

Blank: That was beautiful. It's incredible, because I was going to say exactly the same thing. Sometimes, the best we can do is bear witness, or just be available to hear and be present. That's what we have to offer, and like Loretta said, a computer program, a computer screen, ain't going to do that.

Tech Talk: Cheating Presence or Enhancing It?   53

Kays: It's not the same with a robot. But, I've heard recently that some people think that within a couple years we're going to be replaced by computer-generated holograms. Which may feel like someone is bearing witness, but I think we always have the knowledge in our heads and hearts that it's not a real person.

Sparks: The projections into the future are for me very fanciful and entertaining. But my experience is that the future is never what we think it's going to be. When you look at what in 1950 they thought things would be like in 50 years, we're not there. I've lived long enough to realize that part of my job is to stay grounded, to the best of my ability, and some days it's shaky. Being in the now, being in the present...that's one thing a machine can't do for you.

Kays: Loretta, I know you do a fair number of sessions via video chat. Do you think that is an acceptable proxy? Are we still getting the same human quality we're discussing?

Blank: I've not done screen-to-screen. I've done phone stuff, and I feel like I'm always missing something. I figure if I'm not getting it from them, I'm sure there's something I'm communicating that they're not getting from me. That's my reluctance.

Sparks: I have had a lot of experience working over video chat and on the phone, and I find the experience I have—and that I perceive my clients having—varies as much as they do. There is the same amount of variation when they are sitting in my office. I'm interactive with my clients and I'm very present with them. There are people who find that too hard to adjust to. Not everyone is going to be your dance partner. I take no issue with that. Either I connect or I don't connect. And in the connection, we get our work done. My absolute favorite though is video chat. I do love seeing the face. I love interacting. I have trained myself to be very quiet on the phone because I have to hear differently, more intensely than I do face-to-face or screen-to-screen. I ask about it when the pause is a little bit longer than it would normally be. Sometimes the dog just spilled something on the floor and they were distracted, or sometimes they were taking a deep breath and remembering something.

Kays: You said that you prefer screen-to-screen. Do you mean you prefer it to in the room?

Sparks: No, my real preference is being in the office, where we have a much richer experience of each other. But I believe we can use the screen if otherwise someone couldn't have therapy.

Blank: A client's wife has been trying to find a therapist for herself in metro Boston and has had enormous difficulty because her work schedule is not flexible. She's found a therapist who does only screen time. Apparently this therapist found a company where all they do is FaceTime therapy, which is mind boggling to me.

Sparks: I have four people I see on-screen, and a couple of people I see via phone. One of these people is not that far from me but the traffic is so horrific that it's an hour here and an hour back. That's three hours out of their day, whereas, when we go online and we have a good connection, not just video connection, but we are able to see each other, it's an hour. It's a valuable hour.

Blank: But see, here's the difference. You have and do see people face-to-face over your lifetime as a therapist. These younger therapists—I'm assuming they're younger—they don't have a face-to-face practice. There's no person who ever comes into their office. It's all electronic. I start to wonder, who are they and what does it mean that they don't have a practice where they see people in person?

Kays: What do you think it means? Or, what do you worry it means?

Blank: My judgment is—and it's really a judgment because I don't know—that they're less able to tolerate the anxiety and the unknown that comes with people showing up in your office. Sometimes it isn't comfortable. When somebody is sitting eight feet from you and they start talking in a way, or they start presenting themselves physically in a certain way, it's like, "Whoa." I know I've been anxious and I start to get the sense that these people don't want that. They can't tolerate that. And hence, they do what they do.

Sparks: I have an add-on to that, Damon. I was looking at some letters from people I have supervised over the years. One of the themes I was pleased to see stayed strong is about bringing your humanity into the room. My supervisees panicked because they weren't able to do the textbook therapy they were taught, and no one told them they were going to be unsure. No one ever told them they were going to be anxious. No one ever told them there would be times when they'd think, "What the hell am I supposed to do with *that?*" So, when we talk about this kind of online therapy, and young therapists doing it, I feel it's really different from a seasoned therapist doing it.

Blank: I agree entirely. It's healthy for us as therapists to appreciate the experience we're having in the moment with our clients; and as teachers, or supervisors, or mentors of other therapists, to let them know that. It's healthy to have your experience and it's essential for our clients' healing. They need to see us as human, and see us as overwhelmed, and befuddled and anxious, and not particularly articulate in the moment, because that's life. In a lot of textbooks and training, there's no attention to humanity. It's as if, if you do this protocol, the person's going to get better.

Kays: That leads to another question I wonder about. I get it, if somebody is ill and they can't come to a session, or there's no therapist in their rural town, doing therapy technologically is better than nothing. But then you do hear the stories about, "Oh, I just didn't want to leave work," or, "I wanted to avoid traffic." I wonder—by doing teletherapy in certain circumstances—are we enabling lazy relationships? Are we devaluing relationships and saying, "There shouldn't be much work involved"? That's the opposite of what I've been taught through therapy. I sometimes fear that if we start saying, "Oh yeah, just Skype in, don't drive all the way across town," we are eroding the fabric of relationships.

Sparks: I've heard so many times that if you don't pay for it, or you don't work for it, it's not going to be valuable. But here's the thing: I don't think I've ever paid for any therapy.

Blank: Wow. You didn't? It's incredible for me to hear that, because at some points in my life, I have felt angry and resentful that I've spent a fortune on my own psychotherapy. On the flip side, there are times I feel incredibly proud that, when I first started as a therapist at a day program, I would leave and drive an hour or an hour and 15 minutes to my therapist's office. I went there, one, because I was desperate, and two, because he was a magnificent human being and a great therapist. I'm proud of how hard I worked and how invested I was, and that I have all the fruits of that labor. So, I wonder, just like you're saying, will people lose that, or not have that?

Sparks: I used to drive an hour and 20 minutes, sometimes on a terrible freeway, every Friday to see my analyst. I did that for a long time. I could get into my thoughts on the way and get out of my thoughts on the way back to work. But I didn't pay for it; my health plan paid for it.

Blank: One of the most therapeutic awarenesses that I've ever had was when I left my office at the day program and was driving to my therapist's office, and I would get stuck in rush-hour traffic, and I would go crazy! I would get anxious, angry, irritable, you name it, at all the cars that were in my way, and I would make myself a physical and emotional wreck. And at some point, I realized that if I didn't learn something about myself in this, I was doomed. So, I sat in my car, I lifted my arms in the air and flexed them, and I realized I was the greatest in the world at making myself anxious, irritable, and upset. It was ludicrous but it was so powerful! And I remember going into my therapist's office and telling him this, and he just smiled at me, like, "You got it."

Sparks: Damon, I have to laugh, because I had that same experience on that long drive. Traffic would often be bad. I'd yell at the cars and I'd hit the steering wheel, and I'd go a little whack-a-doodle, and it dawned on me at one point that I had to accept what it was. I didn't have to like it, but I had to accept it. I had to calm down. And then I started thinking, I'm not a very patient person so I'm going to work on my patience on the freeway. I decided patience is a muscle; mine is weak and I'm going to work on it. So, I turned the traffic into my patience teacher and to this day, when I have to wait when I don't want to, I think, "Ah, an opportunity to work on it.'"

Damon, I have a thought. I'm sitting here listening to your voice and listening to your wisdom. I'm absorbing you. I'm hearing it. It means a lot to me, and I think this is what it's like when you're on the phone listening to a therapist you're connected to.

Blank: I feel flattered. The other thing is that for me with you today, for lack of a better term, it's been like love at first sight. There's been something that I got from you that felt so important. Even if I'm not *seeing* you, I got you. I'm holding you. That has tremendous power to me.

Kays: So, we were talking about technology but you both ended up on this idea of connection, what it's about and how we know it's there, and it was moving just to hear how you discussed that with each other.

Sparks: I've heard that 9 million Americans are shut-ins. This is a group that would really benefit from access to therapy online or by phone. I recall a panel at the I & C several years ago, where one of the panelists spoke of a virtual world online called *Second Life*. It wasn't a game but rather a visual, online, simulation of life. The panelist told the story of a couple who had fallen in love on *Second Life*, then met in the real world, and had a real-world marriage. The husband eventually met another woman in *Second Life* and virtually cheated on his wife. They wound up divorcing over this virtual affair. Another presenter was DeeAnna Merz Nagel, who had a psychotherapy office in *Second Life*. She shared that she once got a call from the police station on *Second Life*. They had a woman in their station, an avatar, who was saying she was suicidal. They opened a portal, brought DeeAnna's avatar in to meet the woman's avatar. The real-life woman was indeed suicidal. They connected in *Second Life* then, if I remember correctly, moved to speaking on the phone and eventually to her real-life office.

Kays: I was on a panel about technology and therapy, and one of the people on the panel kept using language like, "Well, those online relationships aren't real relationships." One audience member stood up furious and crying and said, "How *dare* you tell me that my life and that my relationships are not real?" I use the story sometimes in my trainings on social media for therapists because it was so powerful how hurt she felt, and how dismissed. It's such a different way of looking at things.

Blank: When you say that, I am thrilled that technology is available to people. Just because people can't get anywhere, do they not deserve the contact and the relationships and all the juicy stuff that comes with it?

Sparks: What you were saying a few moments ago, Lisa, about how we wound up talking about connection, that's what we're also talking about with regard to technology. The question is, can there be connection with it? I think it has everything to do with how people come together. It's easier to connect in person for most people, and I think it gets more difficult as you move further away from being physically present to one another. But people also build great relationships and great loves by writing letters to each other. So, it really has to do with the depth and quality of what is communicated.

Kays: And that we can't cheat presence. People know when you're being present or not, no matter what the medium is.

Sparks: I think they do.

Wired Shut

Gina Sangster

All along the platform, heads are bowed
as if in prayer. No one speaks or looks
your way, transfixed by pixels,
news bytes and tweets.

Once seated or standing in train cars,
attention rarely wavers, except to
enter or exit. And at day's end,
passengers lean against windows,
screens held aloft, slack-jawed
and motionless, except for one
moving finger.

Toddlers strapped in strollers clutch
devices just their size or borrowed
from a parent's distracted grasp,
anything to keep the peace as
the hypnotic glare of Disney
characters take the place
of real-life travelers.

In a delusional moment, you
feel the urge to speak to someone
until you see the earbuds planted
firmly in each ear, ensuring
a wall of sound, an unknown
stream of music or voices –
Perhaps they're listening to
War and Peace or *Sophie's Choice*.

So you return to your own
cocoon of silence,
the passing thought of no
consequence, soon forgotten.
You unfurl your Sunday *Post*
or flip open the *New Yorker* to
"Talk of the Town" or the latest
long-form journalistic tour de force,
wondering if you look like a throw-
back to some distant time. Your
smart phone, hidden from view,
vibrates with temptation.

This Is My Brain on ADHD

Rebecca Wineland

REBECCA WINELAND studies social work at Catholic University while working remotely as an ADHD coach. She can't wait for her wedding in August and loves to create art and consume literature. For coaching information, you can contact her at: centeringADHD@gmail.com.

What do Justin Bieber's monkey, the origins of the word "napkin," and Census Bureau data from Lancaster, Virginia, have in common? I know way more about them than I should. And why? I read about them on the Internet for hours instead of doing my homework.

Even among psychotherapists, debate persists about whether attention deficit hyperactive disorder is a legitimate diagnosis. As a recipient of this diagnosis, I would argue that I definitely have a problem, but the label "attention deficit" inaccurately portrays my issue. My focus overflows. There is no deficit. My deficiency lies in my ability to mitigate the object of this abundant focus. Neurotypical individuals can, for example, enjoy dinner at a restaurant without listening to the lyrics of the faint background music, enjoying the awkward first date to the left, and evaluating the emotional state of the waiter. Thankfully, my fiancé is no longer offended when I sing along to Beyoncé in the middle of a serious conversation at a restaurant because he understands that I actually can't help it. And, most of the time, I don't even realize what I am doing!

Technology is my overstimulated brain's best friend and mortal enemy. I knew that I would have a tenuous relationship with a smartphone, so I was the last of my friends to transition. My flip phone lasted until the end of 2013. The man at Best Buy laughed at me and called his friend over to look at my ancient device as he told me there was absolutely no way to transfer my contacts. Even then, I wasn't prepared to have infinity in my pocket.

I can be connected to anything, anywhere, at any time. With my overflow of focus, it can be overwhelming. The amount of time I waste on random things of little-to-no consequence disheartens me. I genuinely don't care about Justin Bieber's monkey, but I read nine different articles about it. It is so easy to click link after link, diving deeper and deeper into any rabbit hole on the Internet.

My fiancé is a wonderful human. He's handsome, funny, smart, and currently cooking food for my birthday party. He's also organized, focused, and steady. I hope I don't drive the poor man crazy. A text message saying, "I'm almost ready" could mean I'm walking out the door. It could also mean that I am about to get dressed but don't even know where my shoes are, and I'm also going to watch two James Corden Carpool Karaoke videos before I come outside. When he gets justifiably frustrated, it compounds the shame I already feel from wrestling my brain. We're learning how to navigate it all, and I'm sure we'll continue to keep learning.

Before I owned a smartphone, I wrote multiple poems or songs a week and drew pictures constantly. In the past four years, I have written 16 songs or poems, and 10 blog posts, and draw only when I forget to buy cards for a wedding or birthday. (That means everyone's wedding and birthday.) Abundant stimulation dampens my creativity because it occupies my brain. I no longer need to amuse myself with my own cartoons, stories, or songs; I have easy access to unlimited cartoons, stories, and songs.

But, as I mentioned earlier, technology is also my best friend. I have this great app called 30/30 that helps with my ADHD symptom of time-blindness. On this app, I can set multiple timers that flow seamlessness into each other. I plan out my next three hours and my phone will tell me what to do and how long I have allotted for each activity. I use another timer app called Forest, as well. Forest grows cute cartoon trees and blocks me from using my phone while the timer counts down. Calm is a meditation app, and meditation is supposed to be very helpful for people with ADHD (who have enough discipline to meditate in the first place). The Calm app also helps deflate restless thoughts at night, which is a really common issue for people, and especially people with ADHD. I utilize another app called Moment, which tracks the amount of time I spend on my phone and number of times I pick up my phone every day. It's not always pretty to look at the data, but it's definitely helpful. Finally, my very best ADHD app and biggest life saver is the Tile app. Tiles are small key chains that you can attach to all of your things. Then, you can see where they are from your phone. It's magical. I can call my phone from my wallet. I can call my keys from my phone. I'm still late to everything, but at least I don't tear apart my home looking for my keys every morning!

ADHD, like any other trait, has powerful pros and cons. My inability to eliminate excess stimuli allows me to wonder at the way the dew catches light on a misty morning. My time-blindness gives me the gift of total presence in a good Russian novel as I read until the pages grow dim. ADHD brains synthesize information in unique ways, and this enables me to problem-solve quickly and imaginatively. I lead well, with high empathy and great enthusiasm, and those traits are common in people who share my label.

Learning to put leashes and boundaries on my technology use is difficult but needed and worthwhile. As I learn how to harness technology instead of sinking under the weight of it all, I free my creativity, and I'm able to share it with others. I can research how other ADHD folks are coping with their symptoms, and I learn from them. YouTube videos have brought tears to my eyes as I realize that I am not alone in my issues. I am growing, I am gifted, and I can move forward.

Tech Q&A

These questions come from recent queries to professional listservs. Our panel of guest editors—Lisa Kays, Eileen Dombo, and Rosemary Moulton—responded.

Q: My clients can email me on a secure portal. I keep my comments succinct and try to maintain healthy ethical boundaries. However, when someone sends a long email filled with details and clinical content, other than continuing to encourage them to bring it into session, how do you ethically maintain boundaries without missing or neglecting something that might be urgent?

A: An informed consent for your practice that takes into account social media and technological boundaries and parameters can be helpful as a reference in situations such as these. We each have different boundaries for our practices around technology, just as we do with our office hours or the degrees to which we self-disclose. This document can also be helpful around safety issues that can arise if patients expect us to check on their wellbeing via social media or to monitor email or texts constantly. It's important that we set expectations around this clearly.

Dr. Keely Kolmes has an excellent outline of a social media policy that can be included with your informed consent and will outline for patients the extent to which they can and should contact you electronically, related risks, and how to contact you (or not) during an emergency. You can access her policy example here: drkkolmes.com/social-media-policy/. In this policy, Dr. Kolmes succinctly identifies how she will and will not interact and engage in every form of technology she uses (or doesn't use) with patients, and outlines safety and urgency parameters, such as how often platforms are monitored, when a response can be expected, and what platforms should not be used for urgent or emergency communications.

While having such a document in place does not guarantee that patients will follow it, it does provide two important things:
1. Peace of mind for therapists so they know what they are responsible for monitoring regularly for urgent and emergency situations, and what they are not.
2. A reference for conversations with patients when boundary challenges do arise, such as the one you mention, so that you can refer back and explain why you didn't see or respond to a message at all (if the boundary is that clinical matters are only discussed in session) or in a certain amount of time. This helps de-personalize it for the patient and, over time, can help lead to productive conversations around boundaries, what is behind a patient continuing to send "urgent" matters through a channel she knows will not satisfy her need, alternative plans for support, etc.

One additional note is that a policy such as Dr. Kolmes' is only helpful to the extent that the practitioner feels truly comfortable with the boundaries she has set. It can therefore be a meaningful and important exercise just to explore, first, how you would set these parameters for yourself, and then to review them from year to year as your life circumstances change. I know that my practice and my availability look very different now that I'm married and a mother to a young son than they were when I was single. I imagine they will change again as my son gets older. For some, they may change due to illness or travel priorities. We are all different and there is no right or wrong way to set our practice boundaries, so we must use our authentic selves, needs, and wellbeing as a guide.

It can be helpful to ask yourself, do you have a time that you give yourself permission to not be connected to your practice? If not, why not? Do you wish you had that? Do you need to establish it? If so, what gets in the way? If you do feel constantly tethered to your practice's phone or email, what is that like for you? Is it stressful? Fulfilling? What kind of boundaries and work/life balance are you modeling for your patients, colleagues, and friends?

These are all deeply personal questions and worth exploring so you can be grounded and clear in your own boundaries, which tends to make it easier to enforce and engage around boundaries with patients. —*Lisa Kays*

Q: How do you handle parents who use email or text as a substitute for being in family session, particularly when childcare is an issue?
A: Regardless of the issue—childcare or work or a car accident—address absence directly. There are a thousand explanations one might hear, from financial and logistical "real world" concerns to more emotional or behavioral ones. My approach is to have the family talk about what the absence is like for them. Is there ambivalence about being in therapy or anxiety about what might happen in the session? Do the parents see their presence as essential to their child's progress in therapy, or is therapy like a music lesson or dentist appointment where you drop the child off and let the professional do the work? Does the child whose therapy this is feel neglected due to the needs of the other children who need tending to? Is this a chronic problem in the family? If so, how can it be resolved? What is getting in the way? If there is no solution, how can the family cope?

If finances and logistics are a true concern, texting into a session may be the best option. If, however, there is more of an emotional avoidance or another issue at play, that may not be an appropriate behavior for the therapist to tolerate or to model and encourage. Technology provides a "half-way" means for people to participate in therapy, which may either mask issues or complicate them. It depends on each situation and the clinical issues at hand to know whether a therapist should meet this need or push for fuller engagement. —*Lisa Kays*

Q: Are texts to/from clients considered part of their medical record?
A: Yes. Any communication in any form with or from a patient can be considered part of the medical record. It is important to inform patients of this in your practice's informed consent. —*Lisa Kays*

Q: For those running a small private practice, Medicare exempts us from the requirement to use electronic health records (EHRs). Are there any known penalties for using non-EHR documentation methods?
A: As of 2018, Medicare does not offer incentive payments to mental health professionals for using electronic health records (EHRs) unless they are a non-hospital-based physician, physician assistant, or nurse practitioner. In other words, the vast majority of mental health providers are not required to use EHRs and there are no penalties as such. —*Rosemary Moulton*

Q: I want to offer my Medicare client teletherapy through either phone or secure video chat. Will that be covered?
A: For teletherapy to qualify for reimbursement under Medicare, the client must be lo-

cated at an "authorized originating site" during the session. There are several criteria for authorized originating sites.

First, the site must be located both in a county outside of a Metropolitan Statistical Area and in a rural Health Professional Shortage Area located in a rural census track. It is best to consult the Medicare Telehealth Payment Eligibility Analyzer, available online, to determine if the site address is eligible.

Second, the site must be at one of the following types of health care centers: offices, hospitals, rural health clinics, critical access hospitals (CAH), federally qualified health centers, hospital based or CAH-based renal dialysis centers, skilled nursing facilities, or community mental health centers.

Third, the teletherapy must occur in real time—meaning synchronous (as when speaking on the phone) or asynchronous (as possibly when texting).

And finally, although most mental health professionals are considered eligible for reimbursement, masters-level psychologists (often licensed as professional counselors) are not.

Although you did not ask for my opinion about these reimbursement eligibility criteria, I will share it anyway. In my experience, when it comes to teletherapy, Medicare stinks. A case example to illustrate:

My client Linda, age 52, is on federal disability and has been diagnosed with PTSD, fibromyalgia, and several other chronic illnesses. She's highly motivated in our work together, however her diagnoses can make it challenging to ride the subway or bus to my office. At times she has reluctantly canceled our sessions because of intense pain. On those days of intense pain, she would be an ideal candidate for teletherapy through video sessions. Because she lives in a metropolitan area, and her ideal teletherapy site would be her apartment, Medicare considers our sessions ineligible for reimbursement. Medicare, in my opinion, should expand its teletherapy site eligibility criteria, so that clients like Linda with chronic pain or disability could be better served.

Medicare does reimburse for in-home therapy sessions, but for an hour-long session, with an additional 30 minutes of travel, it is simply not feasible for me and many other psychotherapists with busy schedules.

As practitioners, we should advocate on behalf of our clients and ourselves. Please consider contacting your senators, representatives, and professional advocacy organization to lobby for expansion of Medicare teletherapy reimbursement eligibility rules. —*Rosemary Moulton*

Q: Are there specific types of encryption required to communicate with clients electronically? What if no patient health information (PHI) is included, for example if it's only appointment reminders or scheduling? Are we required to keep copies of electronic communications if they are only appointment scheduling?
A: Organizations like the American Psychiatric Association and the National Association of Social Workers strongly recommend encrypting electronic communication with and information about clients. However, they do not require a specify type of encryption software. It is the responsibility of the clinician to keep up with the latest technology and research its compliance with HIPAA regulations. However, encryption software must be used by both clinician and client and may not be practicable for certain people. The question of whether to use encryption should center around the risk of violating

confidentiality. So, if you are using electronic communication for appointment scheduling only, think about what is being said in that exchange. Is the term "therapy" anywhere in the exchange, or is it a more neutral term such as "meeting" or "appointment" used? Is there any discussion of content being processed in session, or reminders such as "please bring the signed release so I can talk to your psychiatrist" that may reveal mental health treatment? Ask yourself if you need to protect this information and if it would violate confidentiality for someone else to read or have access to this information. Ask yourself how you would handle this information if it was a verbal exchange in a public area. In other words, is this a conversation you would have in front of others? If your phone or computer is hacked, this information becomes public. Finally, NASW and APA recommend you inform all clients that email and text exchanges are not secure forms of communication. Including this in your informed consent and/or a technology use policy, as well as having a direct verbal discussion about it with clients, will demonstrate a concern for your clients' privacy. —*Eileen Dombo*

Q: I have a client who mostly comes to my office for sessions but travels often for her work as a consultant. She does not want to miss sessions when she travels and has requested phone sessions for these times. How do I handle this request? Is this an allowable form of service provision?
A: The answer to this question depends on a number of factors. It will depend on which state your client is visiting for work, how long she will be there, and whether she seeks insurance coverage for those sessions. Many states consider the location of the client, not the clinician, to determine the required licensing. This means that you will not be able to do a phone session without a license from that state, or risk being disciplined for practicing without a license. For example, if you are a social worker and your client is in Ohio, that board of social work requires you to hold a license from them to provide phone therapy to someone in Ohio. They also require both Medicaid and private health insurance companies to pay for these sessions. Other states, such as Iowa, require you to disclose the risks and limits of this method of service provision, but do not require you to hold a license from the state board of social work.

Aside from licensing and regulatory questions, also think about best practices and ethical questions. Does the client benefit from phone sessions? Is there a confidential and secure place for the client to talk with you without distraction? Has the client checked with their insurance provider to determine if these sessions are covered? If they are not covered, do they agree to assume financial responsibility? You may want to create a financial agreement that outlines these differences. Is the client at risk for dissociation, self-harm, or suicide? When someone is travelling for work, they are probably not aware of local mental health resources, so you may want to set up an agreement prior to travel in which the client tells you where they are travelling to and where they are staying. Finally, contact your malpractice insurance provider and ask about coverage in these kinds of situations. Some providers may decide to disqualify you from coverage if you did not let them know beforehand that you were providing services in this manner. —*Eileen Dombo*

Online Education

Kynai Johnson

I HAVE HAD THE HONOR AND PRIVILEGE TO WORK AS ADJUNCT FACULTY WITHIN THE ONLINE COMMUNITY FOR THE PAST THREE YEARS. In my capacity as an online instructor for an MSW program, I teach courses in assessment and diagnosis, and diversity education. These experiences have generated interesting reflection about the culture of online education, including the role of technology therein.

In addition to teaching online, I also teach in-seat courses and facilitate trainings for various learning communities. As an educator, I recognize the importance of infusing varied and engaging learning modalities into these experiences. For kinesthetic learners, I employ icebreakers and experiential learning activities. Auditory learners can rely on lectures and discussions to meet their needs. As a dominantly visual learner myself, I take joy in creating Power Point presentations to illustrate core concepts. To a certain extent, technology takes a supplemental role in these in-seat learning techniques. However, sharing online videos and articles straddles in-classroom and online engagement, unique to the 21st century community learning experience.

This semester I am teaching an in-seat diversity course that focuses on the relationships communities have with privilege and oppression. On the first day of class, I asked my students what their expectations were: "What do you need from this experience so that this class is not a waste of your time?" After a moment of reflection, one of the students shared, "I want to learn how to have *good,* uncomfortable, conversations." In pursuit of this expectation, we have worked collectively to build mutual respect and communal trust. This strong foundation allows us to dive deeply into discussions of privilege and oppression, in a safe space. We have good, uncomfortable conversations. Notably, I teach this course online, too. As such, I have given extensive consideration to how these approaches translate to cyberspace. Building community and trust is essential to any effective learning environment. However, online versus in-seat implementations are very distinct.

As an in-seat instructor, I am positioned to read classroom energy and respond accordingly, promoting dynamic dialogue and spontaneity. By comparison, online education feels decidedly different. Within a single cohort, students live across many different time zones. This

KYNAI JOHNSON RECEIVED HER MSW from Catholic University's National Catholic School of Social Service, where she is currently completing her PhD. Her doctoral studies focus on fostering positive identity formation in social work practice, particularly related to perceptions of sexual orientation, gender identity and expression, race, and ethnicity. Ms. Johnson has worked at LAYC, a nonprofit in Washington, DC, for five years, and she currently serves as the deputy director of the Education and Workforce Department.
kynai@layc-dc.org

factor alone complicates live, collective engagement and spontaneity.

Nevertheless, we have a responsibility to delve further into making technology expand opportunity, for instance by creating online degree options. Whereas varied learning techniques make education accessible for in-seat scholarship, online education promotes a different type of accessibility. Over the years, students have shared how online learning platforms promote education access as they balance competing life commitments such as financial constraints, full-time employment and work schedules, and family caregiving responsibilities.

In my experiences, the online learning environment has been fostered by a virtual learning platform called Blackboard. Throughout the semester, Blackboard creates a forum for student/teacher engagement, assignment submission, and resource sharing. At the beginning of each semester, in an intentional modeling practice, I post a welcome video to students. After sharing a bit about myself and outlining course content for the semester, I challenge students to create their own three-minute video posts. This assignment's intent is twofold. First, it acclimates students to the technology required to engage online, via a low-pressure assignment. Second, it creates an intentional space for students to announce their presence within our developing online community. These videos typically delve into discussions of career changes, family commitments, geographic location, and other life experiences which have brought them to the online platform. The other students within the cohort are encouraged to watch the videos and post responses. These responses generally acknowledge the discovery of previously unknown connections and other resonating reflections. For instance, students might discover that they are on the same coast, have the same clinical interests, or share similar family structures.

Without a doubt, the online platform fosters a different type of social engagement. As the instructor, I regularly post videos to talk through challenging course content. Additionally, I give very descriptive feedback on assignments, doing my best to relay my "voice" through the written word. Ultimately however, the course is driven by individual student motivation.

Notably, the online format permits a different type of risk-taking for learners. There is a certain vulnerability in voicing your opinion in a classroom setting. Online students, however, seem to share their experiences and explore course content in a different, sometimes more uninhibited way. As an example, I have seen students discussing their own trauma histories in the online welcome videos, which has no in-seat parallel. They also appear less inhibited in their weekly role-play videos, an assignment that explores therapeutic techniques in the assessment and diagnosis course. In the absence of in-person social pressures, students more boldly venture into clinical roles. Students benefit from creating role plays within a safe learning environment of their own choosing; most often, their own homes. They can also record and re-record their role plays, only submitting the material they are most comfortable with. I often watch role-play submissions multiple times, giving extensive feedback. I highlight what they have done to promote a strong therapeutic alliance, naming the emerging tools which may still be unintentional in their burgeoning clinical efforts.

Both online and classroom settings foster unique roles for technology in education. Promoting different types of accessibility, there are unique benefits and challenges to online platforms. In the midst of a now steadfast global community, learning to meaningfully engage and educate online feels focal to the future of education.

Fictional Clinical Supervision Notes: Krista Gordon of the TV Show *Mr. Robot*

Mr. Robot is an American TV drama/thriller that first aired on the USA Network in 2015 with hour-long episodes. Its main character, Elliot Alderson, is a computer hacker with mental illness. He meets weekly with psychotherapist Krista Gordon.

In this fictional account of clinical supervision of psychotherapist Krista Gordon, I've taken creative license with the therapist's reactions and responses to her patient, including his diagnosis and medications. Snippets of their sessions are regularly featured on the show, but not entire sessions. I've considered Krista's outward responses on the show and speculated how she might proceed for the rest of each session.

Many of the details about Elliot listed in the first supervision session are not revealed on the show until later in season one. They are, however, true to the show, along with Elliot's words and actions. Details about Krista's personal life are also consistent with the show.

I am writing as if Krista has an established relationship with a clinical supervisor but is just now seeking guidance about her patient Elliot after 11 months of treatment. Viewers of the show do not know whether Krista is pursuing clinical supervision or professional consultations, but given the unusual nature of this case, she definitely should be seeking guidance! The supervision sessions and notes are entirely fictional.

Rosemary Moulton, LICSW, is a gender therapist and EMDR therapist in private practice in Arlington, Virginia, and Washington, DC. Her passions include travel and nature, and on the Big 5 she scores high on the openness to experience dimension. She plans to someday expand her practice to include teletherapy to reach underserved populations of LGBTQIA young adults in rural areas.
rmoultonlicsw@gmail.com

10/23/2015

Patient EA is a 28-year-old single White heterosexual male who works full-time for a cybersecurity firm in midtown and is a computer hacker in his free time. Krista

Mr. Robot, Episode 3. October 12, 2017. USA Network,

has met with him once weekly for 50-minute sessions of psychotherapy and medication management[1] for 11 months per court mandate (related to anger management and physical destruction of previous workplace's Internet servers). Patient reports no memory of this incident. He has a history of angry outbursts and persecutory delusions. Patient has periods of paranoia about men in black following him. Ongoing social isolation and social anxiety. He has difficulty falling and staying asleep and has an irregular appetite with poor eating habits. Patient is reticent about drug use history although reports daily use of caffeine and tobacco. Denies suicidality.

Patient's father died at age 45 of leukemia (caused by exposure to toxic chemicals on the job) when patient was 9 years old. His father tried to keep the cancer a secret, but when he was very ill, patient told his mother of the illness. His father flew into a rage and pushed patient out of the bedroom window; patient suffered a broken arm that at times still aches. He did not have a close relationship with his mother, who was cold and distant and at times physically abusive. Patient said that she was indifferent towards his father's death. They are not in regular contact. His younger sister is active in his life and shares his interest in computers and hacking. Has a childhood female friend who helped get him a job in IT and seems to care about him deeply.

Lives alone and has a pet fish. Interacts with other hackers online but limited face-to-face contact with people in his life. His boss at work regards him positively although admonishes him about not following business dress code.

Attends sessions faithfully and is always on time. Physical appearance is neat and wears a black hooded sweatshirt to every session. Affect is often flat. He avoids eye contact and there are extended silences.

Because patient does not remember the crime he was convicted for—destruction of his employer's computer network servers—Krista suspects he dissociates. Earlier this year, Krista attempted to administer the Dissociative Experience Scale and was met with silence. Her patient avoided eye contact for several minutes and then reported that he was "fine" and "there is nothing to worry about."

Presence of delusions, depressed mood, and history of manic behavior would indicate schizoaffective disorder bipolar type. Krista has made two adjustments to patient's medications as she increased antipsychotic and augmented with mood stabilizer. Since the changes in medication, patient reports decreased anger and paranoid thoughts.

Treatment goals are to reduce incidence of delusions and angry outbursts, maintain medication compliance, and strengthen social support network.

Krista encourages him to connect with others and attend social events. Most recently he said he attended his childhood friend's birthday party at a bar, but Krista suspects he was not entirely truthful about his attendance. Krista expresses optimism that his social anxiety will dissipate as he makes small steps towards participation in society.

Often patient gives one-word answers to Krista's open-ended questions. I explored with Krista her discomfort around silence during sessions. She reports feeling restless and eager to help patient gain insight so as to overcome challenges. We considered strategies of dual awareness to maintain her sense of calm detachment during these moments. Krista agreed to employ these methods and will follow up with me during next supervision session.

---

1 Krista Gordon is introduced on the show as a psychologist who prescribes medications. In the state of New York, where this show takes place, psychologists do not have prescriptive authority.

11/6/2015

I asked Krista about her success in allowing for silences, and she said that she has taken a different, more confrontational approach with patient. Krista recounted their most recent session. When asked, patient said he was not feeling good. Krista asked what was not feeling good, and patient said "everything." Krista pressed him for specifics and he expressed feeling a lack of control in his life. Krista offered empathy. Patient said "he might as well do nothing." Krista related this feeling of not being in control to his father, and how he chose to do nothing when he was battling his cancer. Patient's father could have fought the company that caused his cancer, told people about his diagnosis, or sought better treatment; instead, he did nothing and died in pain and secrecy. Krista suggested that patient's father may have felt like patient does now. Patient said it was different, and Krista agreed, because patient has found options. Krista emphasized patient's power and control over his own life. She said that he doesn't just have to take what life gives him. Krista pressed further for what is going on with him. Patient repeatedly yelled "shut up." She confronted him about the bags under his eyes, his yelling and jitteriness, and regression into old patterns and behaviors. Krista urged him to tell her what is going on with him and said that she can't help him if he keeps her in the dark. He stayed silent for the remaining 11 minutes of the session.

Krista said her focus has shifted to "preventing patient's self-destruction." I reminded her that she does not in fact have control over his wellbeing, and that if he wishes to change, it must be a choice he makes for himself. I asked if Krista could tolerate his choosing not to change, and she admitted that would be difficult for her. Patient is nearing completion of his court-mandated psychotherapy. Krista said she is worried about him not continuing treatment and going off his medication, which might lead to decompensation. Krista agreed to let him know that their work can continue even after the court requirements have been met. Krista expressed a sense of urgency about their work but recognizes that he has the right to self-determination.

11/16/2015

Patient completed mandated treatment of 12 months and signed court attestation paperwork. He made no indication that he wished to continue working with Krista. The following week he showed up at his regular (but unscheduled) time. Krista was available so met with him. I expressed concern that she did not request he schedule an appointment, but Krista said she was worried that he was in crisis, and that he might not return if she turned him away.

Patient confirmed with Krista that confidentiality would be maintained. He then spoke for 5 minutes straight. Patient said that he had been lying to Krista about taking his pills and revealed that he knows she doesn't take her anti-anxiety medication as prescribed either. Krista told me she was taken aback but allowed him to continue while she maintained silence.

He then proceeded to reveal intimate details about her life, which included the coffee she bought that morning, the text she sent her sister, her finances, her possible countertransference with a patient whom he named, the kind of online porn she enjoys watching, and the deep loneliness she has experienced since her divorce four years ago. He admitted to watching her on her webcam at times and said that she too is lonely and cries. Patient said he hacks everyone, including friends and coworkers, and that through this he has helped a lot of people. He said that he wants a way out of loneliness, just like Krista, and asked if that's what Krista wanted to hear.

Krista said that while listening to this patient, she froze, but that she was able to regain her role as psychotherapist seconds after patient divulged this information. She thanked him for his honesty and reflected that it must have been very difficult for him to not only return to treatment but to share this with her. During the rest of the session, the patient appeared relaxed and made eye contact with her periodically, which was unusual for him.

During our supervision session, Krista expressed discomfort to me about patient's disclosure but said that it reflected a real shift in their therapeutic relationship and a willingness to trust her.

Krista has been hacked by her own patient.

I expressed my concern about the patient's extensive violation of her privacy, and about her willingness to continue treatment with him. Krista told me that at first she was shocked at his admission and felt uncomfortable. She said that a part of her wanted to terminate the therapeutic relationship immediately, but another part of her was worried about his safety, and yet another part of her was impressed by this important breakthrough. Because he is not compliant with his medications, he is at a high risk of decompensation and re-offending. Because it is so difficult for him to trust others, she said she must put aside her discomfort and think of his safety and wellbeing first.

I reminded Krista that her patient hacked into her phone and her computer and is now privy to all the details of her life that leave a digital footprint. I advised her that she must explicitly discuss this with her patient on several counts. First, what did he do with that information, and did he share it with others? Second, does he agree to stop monitoring her phone and computer? Third, does he recognize that his behavior has impacted Krista's sense of safety, and their relationship? Fourth, what are Krista's boundaries, and can he agree to respect them?

Clearly, this patient feels truly powerless and unsafe relating to others. At what point, however, is he wielding too much power over others, and harming them? Can he recognize that his actions have caused harm? If they are to truly relate to one another, Krista must share with him the emotional impact of his violation. If he does not apologize, how can they move forward therapeutically?

Also of grave concern is that the confidentiality of other patients has been compromised, as he clearly named Krista's Thursday 2 p.m. patient. If this patient was able to access Krista's calendar, then the privacy of all of her patients has been breached. This breach of privacy must be reported to both the patients affected and the Department of Health and Human Services. Krista said she had not considered this aspect and said she will send letters to each of her patients immediately, informing them that her calendar had been hacked and their names had been revealed. I instructed Krista to list her corrective actions in the letter, in other words, how she plans to keep their information secure going forward.

As a responsible consumer, Krista should also contact her pharmacy. Because this patient was able to hack into Krista's pharmacy, those patients' privacy has also been compromised. I told Krista that she needs to inform her pharmacy that her records were hacked and that their system is vulnerable to other breaches.

Finally, I encouraged Krista to consider termination of treatment with this patient.

Krista replied that since he is at such high risk for decompensation and involvement with law enforcement, she wishes to continue treatment with him. These boundary violations, she said, can be worked through. Krista said he has made such a remarkable breakthrough in being truthful with her, she is not willing to end their therapeutic relationship at this time.

I asked if she understood all of the concerns I raised, and she said yes, and that she would follow all of my recommendations except terminating with the patient.

Before we finished our supervision session, I reviewed the American Psychological Association's (APA) Ethical Principles of Psychologists and Code of Conduct and found that although it does address maintaining patient confidentiality, it does not specifically address a patient hacking a therapist.

11/20/2015

Krista contacted me for an emergency supervision session. Her ex-boyfriend, Michael, revealed that he too had been hacked by Krista's patient back when he and Krista were still dating. Michael indicated that two months ago, her patient hacked him and then blackmailed him into coming clean with Krista. Michael was not his real name, and he was cheating on his wife with several women and escorts. Krista's patient forced Michael to break up with Krista, otherwise he would report Michael to the police for hiring an underage escort. The patient even took Michael's dog. The dog was microchipped, and because her patient took the dog to the vet, there is now evidence of this crime.

Michael had since reported the patient to the police, and their cybercrime division is building a case against EA. Michael implored Krista for help in convicting him and had deduced that he is one of Krista's patients. Michael correctly guessed that her patient had also hacked her.

Michael's life is now in shambles and he wants to bring EA to justice. Krista said that she couldn't talk to Michael about her patient. Krista refused to help and walked away.

I was shocked at this revelation. *Krista's patient hacked her then-boyfriend, blackmailed him, and caused their breakup.*

I asked Krista how she feels now. She was silent for a few moments. Then she said she knows she should feel violated, but that a part of her feels vindicated. Her ex-boyfriend, Michael, lied about everything to her, and it took blackmail for him to be truthful with her. Michael is an awful human being, and she is better off with him gone. Krista also realizes that her "radar is way off." She trusted Michael completely, and he was lying to her the whole time. She sees parallels in her family of origin and plans to seek her own personal psychotherapy.

Krista said she's not sure what to do about her patient. She has not seen her patient since our last meeting, and they have a session scheduled tomorrow.

She knows that her patient committed the crime of blackmail, but she is bound by HIPAA to confidentiality.

It occurred to me during this supervision session that Krista's patient has *committed a crime against Krista.* This goes beyond boundary violation and constitutes cybercrime. Her patient has illegally accessed her computer and online accounts.

To report her patient's cybercrime of hacking into her computer, Krista said, would be a violation of HIPAA. Hacking is not in itself a violent act, so would not be subject to the Tarasoff standards of duty to warn.

I asked Krista what her reluctance was in seeing herself as a victim of her patient. She said that any suffering she has endured is outweighed by her concern for her patient's safety and wellbeing. "You're different than most. At least you try," is what her patient said to her during their last session. Krista said she has worked over a year to build his trust. If she were to terminate with him, she would be abandoning him and putting him at even greater risk for decompensation and further court involvement.

To the best of my knowledge, Krista has not violated her professional ethics code, but her patient's invasion of her privacy is a boundary crossing that cannot be tolerated. He has trespassed. He has barged through what should have been closed doors and has watched Krista cry. He knows what porn she watches online, for heaven's sake. I asked Krista why this was acceptable to her, and she replied that her focus was entirely on her patient's safety, and not on her own.

Once again I reviewed the APA Ethical Principles of Psychologists and Code of Conduct and found that "psychologists may terminate therapy when threatened or otherwise endangered by the client/patient or another person with whom the client/patient has a relationship." I shared this with Krista and explained to her that she is well within her right to terminate treatment with this patient.

Krista thanked me for my feedback, and she has made the decision to address the boundary violation of her personal information. She does not plan to reveal her knowledge of the patient's interference in her life.

I suggested we role-play the conversation, and Krista said she knows exactly what to say and how to say it. She smiled and thanked me again.

12/4/2015

Krista and I were scheduled for a supervision session, but she did not show or call. I called both her cell phone and office phone and got no answer. I sent her an email expressing concern and asked if she wished to reschedule. I received no reply.

1/8/2016

On 12/25/15 I received a reply to my email about our missed session. Krista apologized but made no mention of rescheduling. I replied with concern about patient EA and let her know that she should continue to seek supervision about her work with him.

Her patient said he hacks everyone. He hacked Krista and Krista's boyfriend. Might he also hack her professional colleagues? Have I been hacked by her patient? I will no longer communicate with Krista via email.

1/29/2016

After having received no response from Krista, through phone or email, I mailed Krista a letter of termination. I will no longer be providing her clinical supervision. In my letter, I strongly recommended that she seek ongoing supervision regarding this patient's treatment.

Fantasy and Therapy: Psychotherapists on the Not-So-Blank Screen

Jonathan Farber

JONATHAN FARBER, PHD, provides individual and group psychotherapy and offers private supervision in both Washington, DC, and Chapel Hill, North Carolina. He was trained in clinical psychology at Duke University, taught at UNC-Chapel Hill, and has been practicing privately for over 35 years. He decries the profusion of acronyms in psychotherapy, as well as the trend towards manualized psychotherapy which deemphasizes the uniqueness of the individual, and the power of the unique elements present in each therapeutic relationship.
jonathan.farber@gmail.com

FANTASY WORKS WONDERS. Fantasy, per psychodynamic theory, keeps us in emotional balance. In our fantasies, we escape situations that frustrate us, take merciless and guiltless revenge on our persecutors, master skills without tedious practice, savor mass adulation without triggering our public speaking anxiety, challenge authorities without consequences, or move on from our losses without grief-work.

TV and cinema are technology that provide us with pre-programmed fantasies; we don't even have to concoct our own. The human themes are common enough that the same fantasies appeal to millions. It's a great technology.

Crime and punishment dramas, for instance, are exceedingly popular on screen, as they have been in print: just consider how many forms of emotional gratification they provide. We viscerally enjoy the release of committing the crime—the acting-out of aggression—by covertly identifying with the killer, while at the same time we identify with the righteous innocence of the victim. Eventually we enjoy the reassuring restoration of order and morality, when justice is done, and even take pleasure in the socially sanctioned and morally acceptable aggression against the perpetrator. The comforting takeaway, of which so many viewers seem never to tire, is that aggression—which plagues us all from within—can be safely managed.

Therapists have long attracted Hollywood attention for obvious reasons: the perceived power and influence, the proximity to madness (usually, the patient's), the therapists' own experience of the anxiety that goes with carrying so much trust and responsibility, and of course, the potential for a dramatic redemption narrative if the therapy is successful. On the other hand, to a director composing a scene, the most boring, to be avoided-at-all-costs portrayal is "talking heads," where the screen is simply face shots of two people conversing. That is why therapy scenes themselves tend to be very brief on screen, even when therapy is at the center of the plot. Here are some therapists from the screen who have attracted my attention, and some thoughts about why they are portrayed in the ways that they are.

Hollywood feels free to portray therapeutic events unrealistically, in the interest of entertainment, and sometimes the divergence between clinical reality and movie reality is instructive. Let's look at three examples of boundary violations in the movies: in *Prince of Tides,* therapist Barbara Streisand has a sexual relationship with her patient's brother. In *Good Will Hunting,* Robin Williams roughs up his patient, physically, when Matt Damon challenges his late wife's good name. In *House of Games,* Lindsay Crouse plays a therapist who attempts to rescue her patient from his gambling crises by participating in his life outside the consultation room, and she is insidiously drawn into the thrills of his dangerous lifestyle and multi-layered con games. In each of these films, I expect, audiences largely affirmed the therapist's choices, while therapists in the audience cringed. In the more recent television series *Gypsy,* most of the dramatic tension revolves around the therapist's emotional instability and egregious boundary violations too numerous to list. It is morally edgy in the sense that we the audience are kept on the line between being frightened for the therapist and being judgmental of her. In spite of the strong acting, the plot line is so absurd and melodramatic that I personally could not remain engaged.

Usually, on screen, therapists are morally simple characters—simply good, like the warm and steadfast Judd Hirsch in *Ordinary People,* or simply evil, like the sexually twisted Michael Caine in *Dressed to Kill,* or simply befuddled, like kind-hearted Bob Newhart. Psychiatrists are often seen as having special power within the medical system. There is the henpecked Dr. Spivey, in *One Flew over the Cuckoo's Nest,* who is putty in the hands of Nurse Ratchet, the real power on the psych ward. This echoes the larger theme of the film, that the wrong people are in charge. There is Dr. Silberman, the cowardly bully in *Terminator 2,* who literally punishes Sarah Connor for what he believes are her delusions, as if this will cure her. And there is the psychiatrist played by Paul Reiser in the recent TV series *Stranger Things,* who imprisoned, exploited, and deceived children born with psionic gifts, but who ultimately redeems himself when he sacrifices his own life in the battle to save humanity from alien invaders. Outside the hospital realm, though, Hollywood focuses on the foibles and ordinary human weaknesses of psychiatrists, as in the two brothers in *Fraser,* one of whom is a Freudian with a call-in radio show, the other a Jungian in private practice, but both of whom are loving and lovable, as well as neurotic and bumbling—basically reincarnated Bob Newharts.

One on-screen therapist with moral complexity is portrayed in one of the few shows that also has extended therapy scenes. Gabriel Byrne of *In Treatment* sometimes seemed so authentic I simply couldn't watch it: "I had enough of this crap at the office today," I'd tell my wife. In entertainment, apparently, I need enough verisimilitude that I can at least partly believe what I'm watching. But there is no point in watching something that is *too* much like daily reality: it's more of the workday, and you don't even get paid.

Another more complex therapist, in a show with more extended therapy scenes, is

Tony's therapist, Dr. Melfi, on *The Sopranos*. She has a complex relationship with her sociopathic patient, sometimes wishing to help him, sometimes feeling attracted to him, sometimes feeling repelled by him, and her struggles with alcohol add another layer of complexity. When she is raped and her assailant goes free on a technicality, she faces the temptation of telling her patient Tony, knowing that he would exact extra-legal revenge. She also refers Tony's wife, Carmela, to an older colleague, who refuses to take her "blood money" and apparently believes both Carmela and Melfi should end their respective relationships with Tony. Like *In Treatment,* there are boundary violations, but they are believable, because the therapists involved appreciate how serious they are. I couldn't enjoy this one either, not because the therapy was too realistic, but because its uniformly dark portrayal of a seamy underworld left me with no characters to actually like.

On the other hand, a therapist on the front lines whom I'd urge every therapist to see is James Coburn as *The President's Analyst,* a therapist who goes missing in an elaborate 1960s spoof of the conventional thriller, *The President's Plane is Missing*. We meet Coburn grumbling to himself that everyone in the world except him, the president's analyst, has someone they can talk to, because no one has sufficient security clearance to be his therapist. He's kidnapped by spies from one country after another in a romp that includes drugs, itinerant hippies, rock and roll, and free love, in the course of which he bravely makes his own self-discoveries. Ultimately two superspies from opposite sides in the cold war, a KGB agent and a CIA agent, unite to save him because Coburn, their prisoner, has started therapy with them, and they are suddenly in touch with how unhappy they are and how badly they need to finish their therapy. The ultimate villain—pulling all the strings behind all the villains—turns out to be (drumroll, please)...The Phone Company (TPC), which wants Coburn to convince the president that every citizen should have a phone implanted in their brain while still *in utero*. It's a prescient vision from 50 years ago of our terrifyingly networked contemporary lives, and the invasion of the therapeutic relationship in the film is a wonderful image for the death of privacy. And it's delightful and indulgent for us, as therapists, to see a colleague on screen bravely facing his own inner fears while experiencing the richness of life in the emerging counterculture, and then taking action to save the world. It's a great fantasy wish-fulfillment for therapists. Treat yourself to it.

Here are two changes I've noticed over time in Hollywood's portrayals of therapists. One is that there are no longer so many hostile jokes about how much money therapists make. Sadly, I think that—relative to other professions—we've plummeted in average income. Apparently in response to insurance companies seeking to drive down their costs by flooding the market with therapists, licensing laws have been drastically changed, and most psychotherapy now is done by therapists with fewer years of formal training and less advanced degrees than a generation ago. This has not been all bad. Therapists are shaped far more by their personalities and life experiences than by formal training anyway, and one could legitimately question whether additional years in the classroom or the library actually make us better at psychotherapy. Consistent with the reduced education and the reduced pay, therapist-client relationships, on and off screen, have become less formal than they were. Therapists who behave or are perceived as authority figures have become rare, which I expect helps the therapeutic process more than it impairs the outcome, with most clients.

The other change is that the Hollywood staple, the idealized sincere and competent male therapist, usually Jewish, has disappeared, which I confess leaves me personally with a sense of regret. Judd Hirsch in *Ordinary People,* Sydney Sheldon on *MASH,* and Adam Arkin on *West Wing* seem to be from a different era. Strength and kindness no longer seem to coexist in a male character, and certainly not in a therapist. The culture of Hollywood, like the culture of psychotherapy, has moved on. Although male authority is no longer respected nor trusted, there apparently remains an inextinguishable hunger for father figures—for male authority—and we can wonder whether this might be part of the explanation for the astonishing choice to elect a male president who was neither trusted nor respected by most of us. With this last statement, you might think that this essay has moved beyond the issues of the screen. I wish that were true, but for most of us, national politics is also primarily encountered on the same screen as movies and film, and we are subject to manipulation by the same technical variables: face and voice, script and camera work. In national politics, however, the stakes are ominously different. ▼

The real problem is not whether machines think, but whether men do.
—B. F. Skinner

Tom Burns

Rearview Mirror—A Fantasy

If I were gathering parts of a therapist from TV and movies I knew when I was 18, my ideal therapist would have been a mix of behaviors and attitudes from the Williams, Newhart, Streisand and Hirsch portrayals: counselors Maguire, Hartley, Lowenstein and Berger. My therapist would answer to "Sal" and be available from week-to-week, one minute to the next and between sessions. We'd share an oceanic oneness and wallow in blissful dependency.

Committed to adolescent projections of fear and inadequacy, I'd deal in one-liners attacking Sal and his artwork. He'd pin me against the wall—by the throat even, and that'd happen maybe once or twice a year. I'd wear some kind of harness under my clothing so that the force he exerted would disperse across my chest and back, and chafe with just a little bruising. Sal would also wear the same kind of getup. As therapy moved along, I'd jack him up against the wall when I noticed any arrogance or piss-poor managing of transference. Like if he tried to match my one-liners. "Sal," I'd say, "I'm the asshole here!" We would laugh hard afterwards. Tearful—sad and happy. He'd chafe and bruise, too.

Sal would tell me I needed group therapy. In group he'd straight-up confront ridiculous assertions, compulsions, and feelings with his own ridiculous shtick, and yell, "Quit it!" When the group got slow we'd persuade him to do a lame standup routine, which somehow seemed funny back in the '70s. He'd hold pretend phone calls, and his end of the conversation, the part we heard, would be witty and dry. Then, mocking, I'd say, "Quit it!" He'd invite an unhappy clown to join the group and a ventriloquist whose dummy wanted to abandon the act.

Tom Burns, PhD, lives and practices as a therapist in Northeast Tennessee. He is engrossed by his daughters and granddaughters, poetry, and anticipation of an overseas trip with his wife. His preferred media are the pod sphere and yes,Twitter.
burnsvoices@gmail.com

Identifying with the dummy, I'd try to persuade everyone to drop out of group. "Sal's a dick," I'd say. "Let's get the fuck out of here!" And we would.

At times Sal would be a woman. She'd sit on the edge of her chair and push me to stay with feelings. Somehow I'd recognize that, unlike the movies, she'd neither seduce nor be seduced while listening to an 18-year-old's fantasies. Sal could contain whatever I threw at her, but feigning indifference, I'd speak only of superficial shit. Nothing about what was happening in the room, between us. She would oppose my wish to terminate. "I'm cured!" I'd say—my gambit to avoid speaking of what they call "libidinal fantasies," or really anything significant. But then I'd be all-in with the libido. In my dreams. And I would suggest we go out for coffee. We'd sit too close. I'd feel shame.

Finally, in his Judd Hirsch persona, Sal would permit an office visit in the middle of the night after I'd called him, desperate with self-loathing, guilt and despair. "You've found me," I'd mutter. Astonished by his steadfastness, I'd be queasy with joy. Aware we were both in the same film.

Technology is cool, but you've got to use it as opposed to letting it use you.
—Prince

Are you there?
Kathryn Van der Heiden

Between you and me
Infinite space
Across from one another
Cell phones lightening up our faces
Sharing texts
Bits of conversations
Snap chats
Breathing autonomously
No effort
No consciousness
Time passes
We don't look up very often
Silence is not our friend
We are quick to anticipate
What might come if we sit quietly
In one another's presence
Any silence is too hard to bear
We long for more distraction
The illusion of communication
That we are connected
We share the small things,
The funny things
The sound bites
We notice the absence
When we lay our phones down
Your eyes barely meet mine
What color are they anyway?
Sound bites are predictable
If not very filling
I am hungry for the sound of your voice
I miss you but I don't know how to talk to you
In real time
I wonder if I really even know you?
I wonder if I really even know myself.
I am lost in the distraction in which I choose to live

Editor's note: The AAP Tape Library is a collection of 103 sound recordings of therapists working in session, demonstrating in role-plays, and speaking at workshops, mostly in the mid-20th century. The tapes and their transcripts have recently been digitized and eventually will be accessible by AAP members; a copy is in the Library of Congress as well. Voices here begins an occasional offering of an unedited transcript along with commentaries by current members. Carl Rogers became AAP's first president in 1956.

AAP Tape Library

Tape #3: Carl Rogers
Mr. Vac

By Carl R. Rogers, PhD
University of Wisconsin

For some time I have been frustrated in knowing how to communicate some of the new learnings in which a group of us have been involved in our work with hospitalized schizophrenic clients. As a part of a large research program whose rationale and instrumentation are described elsewhere (1, 2) we have been dealing with schizophrenic individuals selected to be representative of the hospital population. It means that we have been dealing, not with those schizophrenics regarded as promising for therapy, or those whose prognosis is good, but with a representative sample. It means that we have been dealing quite largely with individuals who do not know what psychotherapy is, who probably would not choose it if they did know, who are often of low socio-educational status, who feel no conscious need for help. It is an understatement to say that this is an exceedingly difficult group with whom to work.

While we have not always been successful we have been making genuine progress in working with these often reluctant clients. We have learned to put ourselves into the relationship, in a way which does not impose on the client, but clearly offers him a relationship. We have learned to extend our empathic responses not only to every verbal expression but, as in play therapy, to every unverbalized and non-verbal cue to which we can be sensitive. We have learned to put ourselves, as feeling human beings, into the relationship—again, in ways that do not impose. I think we have made significant strides, of real theoretical as well as practical importance, in broadening our way of operating in psychotherapy. To me it seems like a further forwards step in the development of a therapy which respects the client, builds on his motivation, and facilitates the experiencing of his deepest feelings.

So I have wished to communicate this developing trend to those who are interested in psychotherapy. There are already plenty of recorded or filmed examples of our way of working with the non-hospitalized clinic client. In 1942 I published the first complete transcribed case. In 1952 I made available on film a first interview with a student and a later interview with an adult woman (3). Although the sound tracks were not very adequate, these constituted a pioneering venture. In 1955 I completed films, available to the professional public, of a first interview with a young man, and an interview with a young woman deeply involved in the process of therapy (4, 5). Each of these are complete, unedited interviews and they are available on LP recordings (6) as well as on film. Since that time, through the American Academy of Psychotherapists, I have made available tapes of interviews with other individuals. In addition, many other recordings have been used for teaching purposes, so that it is evident there is no hesitation on my part in making available, for professional scrutiny and consideration, every aspect of our therapeutic work.

But in the work we are doing with schizophrenic individuals I was held back by one hard but simple fact. The "interviews" were mostly silence. When perhaps 40 of the 45 minutes of a contact is made up of complete silence, it is not very feasible to use this as an illustration of therapy, even if the five expressive moments are significant. So it seemed quite impossible to acquaint the professional group with these new—and to us exciting—trends.

The present tape is one attempt to surmount this barrier. I have simply clipped out the silences, reducing every silence to 15 seconds, no matter what its real length. The transcript, however, indicates the number of seconds or minutes eliminated, and whenever the period is longer than two minutes the time has been underlined, to call attention to the fact that a really long silence has intervened. For this reason it is important to have the transcript in hand when listening to the tape. Because this omission of the silences has greatly shortened the tape, it has been possible [to] present two consecutive interviews on one tape, which runs for approximately 40 minutes.

Now a few words of introduction to Mr. Vac (pseudonym, of course), the client in these interviews. He is a presentable appearing young man in his late twenties, who has been hospitalized for three separate periods. The first two periods of hospitalization were for three months and two months, respectively, but the present commitment has already lasted for two years and one month. He is an intelligent individual, having completed high school and taken a little college work. The hospital diagnosis was schizophrenic reaction, simple type.

His case history contains, I am sure, an account of his developing difficulties and of the reasons for his hospitalizations. Since I have carefully avoided looking at this case history, I cannot give you these details. I might say, to alleviate the shock I am undoubtedly giving to the diagnostically oriented by this statement, that had I been trying to determine if he was a promising candidate for psychotherapy, I would have studied the background material. Since however he was one of a matched pair in our research, and the fact that he was to be offered therapy was determined by the flip of a coin, this issue was already settled. And since I was to try to make a therapeutic relationship available to him, I preferred to attempt to do this in terms of what he *is in the relationship,* rather than in terms of his case history.

I seriously considered studying his case history in order to summarize it for this document, but I felt it would be misleading, even though I recognize that it makes many psychologists and psychiatrists acutely uncomfortable to approach a person without having a solid picture of his history in mind. But since I met him without knowing his background, I am asking you to do the same. Since it is my conviction that therapy (if it takes place at all) takes place in the immediate moment-by-moment interaction in a relationship, I am asking you to endeavor to look at it that way as well. (I trust that you will feel it is an interaction, even though Mr. Vac's total verbalization in the first hour runs to a trifle over 50 words—about the right length for a Western Union night letter!)

At the time of these two interviews, I had been seeing Mr. Vac on a twice-a-week basis (with the exception of some vacation periods) for a period of 11 months. Unlike many of our clients in this research, the relationship had, almost from the first, seemed to have some meaning to him. He had ground privileges, so he was able to come to his appointments, and he was almost always on time, and very rarely forgot them. The relationship between us was good. I liked him and I feel sure that he liked me. Rather early in our interviews he muttered to his ward physician that he had finally found someone who understood him. He was never articulate, though this was slightly changed when he was expressing anger, when he could talk a bit more freely. He had, previous to these interviews, worked through a number of his problems, the most important being his facing of the fact that he was entirely rejected by his stepmother, relatives, and worst of all, by his father. During a few interviews preceding these two he had been even more silent than usual, and I had no clue to the meaning of his silence.

In the two interviews presented here I was endeavoring to understand all that I possibly could of his feelings. I had little hesitancy in doing some empathic guessing, for I had learned that though he might not respond in any discernible way when I was right in my inference, he would usually let me know by a negative shake of his head if I were wrong. Mostly, however, I was simply trying to be [with] my feelings in relationship to him, and in these particular interviews my feelings I think were largely those of interest, gentleness, desire to understand, compassion, eagerness to stand with him in his despairing experiences.

To me any further introduction would be superfluous. I hope and believe that the recording of the two hours speaks for itself of many convictions, operationally expressed, about psychotherapy.

References Mentioned

1. Rogers, C. R. The process of personality change in schizophrenics during psychotherapy. A proposal for research. In *Symposium on Psychotherapy with Schizophrenics,* University of Louisiana Press (In press.)
2. Rogers, C. R. A study of psychotherapeutic changes in schizophrenics and normals: The design and instrumentation paper given to Regional Research Conference, American Psychiatric Association, October, 12, 1960.
3. Rogers, C. R. and Segel, R. H. *Client-centered Therapy I and II*. Films distributed by Psychological Cinema Register, State College, Pennsylvania, 1952.
4. Rogers, C. R. and Segel, R. H. *Psychotherapy begins: the Case of Mr. Lin.* Film distributed by Psychological Cinema Register, 1955.
5. Rogers, C. R. and Segel, R. H. *Psychotherapy in Process: The Case of Miss Mun.* Film distributed by Psychological Cinema Register, 1955.
6. LP recordings of the above two interviews. Available through Dr. James Berlin, 1402 University Avenue, Madison, Wisconsin.

The Tuesday Interview

T: I see there are some cigarettes here in the drawer. Would you care for one? Hum? Yeah, it is hot out.

(Silence of 25 seconds has been eliminated from the tape)

T: Do you look kind of angry this morning, or is that my imagination? Not angry, huh?

(Silence of 1 minute, 26 seconds has been eliminated from the tape)

T: Feel like letting me in on whatever is going on?
 (Silence of 12 minutes, 52 seconds has been eliminated from the tape)
T: I kind of feel like saying that "If it would be of any help at all I'd like to come in." On the other hand if it's something you'd rather... if you just feel more like being within yourself, feeling whatever you're feeling within yourself, why that's okay too... I guess another thing I'm saying, really, in saying that is, "I do care. I'm not just sitting here like a stick."
 (Silence of 1 minute, 11 seconds has been eliminated from the tape)
T: And I guess your silence is saying to me that either you don't wish to or can't come out right now and that's okay. So I won't pester you but I just want you to know, "I'm here."
 (Silence of 17 minutes, 41 seconds has been eliminated from the tape)
T: I see I'm going to have to stop in a few minutes.
 (Silence of 20 seconds has been eliminated from the tape)
T: It's hard for me to know how you've been felling, but it looks as though part of the time maybe you'd rather I didn't know how you were feeling. Anyway it looks as though part of the time it just feels very good to let down and—relax the tension. But as I say I don't really know... how you feel. It's just the way it looks to me. Have things been pretty bad lately?
 (Silence of 45 seconds has been eliminated from the tape)
T: Maybe this morning you just wish I'd shut up... And maybe I should but I just keep feeling I'd like to, I don't know, be in touch with you in some way.
 (Silence of 2 minutes, 21 seconds has been eliminated from the tape)
 (Mr. Vac yawns)
T: Sounds discouraged or tired.
 (Silence of 41 seconds has been eliminated from the tape)
C: No. Just lousy.
T: Everything's lousy, huh? You feel lousy?
 (Silence of 39 seconds has been eliminated from the tape)
T: Want to come in Friday at 12 at the usual time?
 (He yawns and mutters something unintelligible)
 (Silence of 40 seconds has been eliminated from the tape)
C: No. I just ain't no good to nobody, never was, and never will be.
T: Feeling that now, huh? That you're just no good to yourself, no good to anybody. Never will be any good to anybody. Just that you're completely worthless, huh?... Those really are lousy feelings. Just feel that you're no good at *all*, huh?
C: Yeah. That's what this guy I went to town with just the other day told me.
T: This guy that you went to town with really told you that you were no good? Is that what you're saying? Did I get that right?
C: Uh, hum.
T: I guess the meaning of that if I get it right is that here's somebody that... meant something to you and what does he think of you? Why, he's told you that he thinks you're no good at *all*. And that just really knocks the props out from you.
 (He weeps quietly)
T: It just brings the tears.
 (Silence of 20 seconds has been eliminated from the tape)
 (Voices from corridor in the background)

C: I don't care though.
T: You tell yourself you don't care at all, but somehow I guess some part of you cares because some part of you weeps over it.

(Silence of 19 seconds has been eliminated from the tape)

T: I guess some part of you just feels, "Here I am hit with another blow, as if I hadn't had enough blows like this during my life when I feel that people don't like me. Here's someone I've begun to feel attached to and now he doesn't like me. And I'll say I don't care. I won't let it make any difference to me… But just the same the tears run down my cheeks."
C: I guess I always knew it.
T: Hm?
C: I guess I always knew it.
T: If I'm getting that right, it is that what makes it hurt worst of all is that when he tells you you're no good, well shucks, that's what you've always felt about yourself. Is that… the meaning of what you're saying? …Uh, hum, so you feel as those he's just confirming what… you've already known. He's confirming what you've already felt in some way.

(Silence of 23 seconds has been eliminated from the tape)

T: So that between his saying so and your perhaps feeling it underneath, you just feel about as no good as anybody could feel.

(Silence of 2 minutes, 1 second has been eliminated from the tape)

T: And I sorta let it soak in and try to feel what you must be feeling… it comes up sorta this way in me and I don't know—but as though here was someone you'd made a contact with, someone you'd really done things for and done things with. Somebody that had some meaning to you. Now, wow! He slaps you in the face by telling you you're just no good. And this really cuts so deep, you can barely stand it.

(Silence of 30 seconds has been eliminated from the tape)

T: I've got to call it quits for today, Vac.

(Silence of 1 minute, 18 seconds has been eliminated from the tape)

T: It really hurts, doesn't it?

(Silence of 26 seconds has been eliminated from the tape)

T: I guess if the feelings came out you'd just weep and weep and weep.

(Silence of 1 minute, 3 seconds has been eliminated from the tape)

T: Help yourself to some Kleenex if you'd like… Can you go now?

(Silence of 23 seconds has been eliminated from the tape)

T: I guess you really hate to, but I've got to see somebody else.

(Silence of 20 seconds has been eliminated from the tape)

T: It's really bad, isn't it?

(Silence of 22 seconds has been eliminated from the tape)

T: Let me ask you one question and say one thing. Do you still have that piece of paper with my phone number on it and instructions, and so on? Okay. And if things get bad, so that you just feel real down, you have them, call me. 'Cause that's what I'm here for, to try to be of some help when you need it. If you need it, you have them. Call me.
C: I think I am beyond help.
T: Huh? Feel as though you're beyond help. I know. Feel just completely hopeless about yourself. I can understand that. I don't feel hopeless but I can realize that you do. Just feel as though nobody can help you and you're really beyond help.

(*Silence of 2 minutes, 1 second has been eliminated from the tape*)
T: I guess you just feel so, so down that… it's just awful.
(*Silence of 2 minutes has been eliminated from the tape*)
T: I guess there's one other thing too. I, I'm going to be busy here this afternoon till four o'clock and maybe a little after. But if you should want to see me again this afternoon, you can drop around about four o'clock. Okay? …Otherwise I'll see you Friday at noon. Unless I get a call from you. If you, if you're kind of concerned for fear anybody would see that you've been weeping a little, you can go out and sit for a while where you waited for me. Do just as you wish on that. Or go down and sit in the waiting room there and read magazines… I guess you really have to go.
C: Don't want to go back to work.
T: You don't want to go back to work, hm?
(*This is the end of the interview. Later in the day the therapist [saw] Mr. Vac on the hospital grounds. He seemed much more cheerful and said he thought he could get a ride into town that afternoon…*
The next time the therapist saw Mr. Vac was three days later, on Friday. This interview follows.)

The Friday Interview

T: I brought a few magazines you can take with you if you want.
(*Silence of 47 seconds has been eliminated from the tape*)
T: I didn't hear from you since last time. Were you able to go to town that day?
C: Yeah. I went in with a kid driving the truck.
T: Uh, hum.
(*Voices from the next office*)
(*Silence of 2 minutes has been eliminated from the tape*)
T: Excuse me a minute.
(*Therapist goes to stop noise*)
(*Silence of 2 minutes, 20 seconds has been eliminated from the tape*)
T: I don't know why, but I realize that somehow it makes me feel good that today you don't have your hand up to your face so that I can somehow kind of see you more. I was wondering why I felt as though you were a little more here than you are sometimes and then I realized well, it's because… I don't feel as though you're hiding behind your hand, or something.
(*Silence of 50 seconds has been eliminated from the tape*)
T: And I think I sense, though I could be mistaken, I think I do sense that today just like some other days when you come in here, it's just as though you let yourself sink down into feelings that run very deep in you. Sometimes they're very bad feelings like last time and sometimes probably they're not so bad, though they're sort of… I think I understand that somehow when you come in here it's as though you do let yourself down into those feelings, and now…
C: I'm gonna take off.
T: Huh?
C: I'm gonna take off.
T: You're going to take off? Really run away from here? Is that what you mean? Must be

some, what's, what's the... what's the background of that? Can you tell me? Or I guess what I mean more accurately is I know you don't like the place but it must be that something special came up or something?
C: I just want to run away and die.
T: Uh, hum. Uh, hum. Uh, hum. It isn't even that you want to get away from here *to* something. You just want to leave here and go away and die in a corner, huh?
(Silence of 30 seconds has been eliminated from the tape)
T: I guess as I let that soak in I really do sense how, how deep that feeling sounds, that you, I guess the image that comes to my mind is sort of a, a wounded animal that wants to crawl away and die. It sounds as though that's kind of the way you feel that you just want to get away from here and, and vanish. Perish. Not exist.
(Silence of 1 minute has been eliminated from the tape)
C: All day yesterday and all morning I wished I were dead. I even prayed last night that I could die.
T: I think I caught all of that, that... for a couple of days now you've just *wished* you could be dead and you've even prayed for that... I guess that. The one way this strikes me is to live is such an awful thing to you, you wish you could die, and not live.
(Silence of 1 minute, 12 seconds has been eliminated from the tape)
T: So that you've been just wishing and wishing that you were not living. You wish that life would pass away from you.
(Silence of 30 seconds has been eliminated from the tape)
C: I wish it more'n anything else I ever wished around here.
T: Uh, hum. Uh, hum. Uh, hum. I guess you've wished for lots of things but boy! It seems as though this wish to not live is deeper and stronger than anything you've ever wished before.
(Silence of 1 minute, 36 seconds has been eliminated from the tape)
T: Can't help but wonder whether it's still true that some things this friend said to you— are those still part of the thing that makes you feel so awful?
C: In general, yes.
T: Uh, hum.
(Silence of 47 seconds has been eliminated from the tape)
T: The way I understand that is that in a general way the fact that he felt you were no good has just set off a whole flood of feeling in you that makes you really wish, wish you weren't alive. Is that... somewhere near it? I ain't no good to nobody, or I ain't no good to nothing, so what's the use of living?
T: Uh, hum. You feel, "I'm not good to another living person, so... why should I go on living?"
(Silence of 21 seconds has been eliminated from the tape)
T: And I guess a part of that is that, here I'm kind of guessing and you can set me straight, I guess a part of that is you felt, "I tried to *be* good for something as far as he was concerned. I really tried. And now... if I'm no good to him, if he feels I'm no good, then that proves I'm just no good to anybody." Is that, uh... anywhere near it?
C: Oh, well, other people have told me that too.
T: Yeah. Uh, hum. I see. So you feel if, if you go by what others... what several others have said, then, then you are *no good*. No good to anybody.
(Silence of 3 minutes, 40 seconds has been eliminated from the tape)

T: I don't know whether this will help or not, but I would just like to say that... I think I can understand pretty well... what it's like to feel that you're just no damn good to anybody, because there was a time when... I felt that way about *myself*. And I know it can be *really rough*.
   (Silence of 13 minutes has been eliminated from the tape)
T: I see we've only got a few more minutes left.
   (Silence of 2 minutes, 51 seconds has been eliminated from the tape)
T: Shall we make it next Tuesday at 11, the usual time?
   (Silence of 1 minute, 35 seconds has been eliminated from the tape)
T: If you gave me an answer, or not, I really didn't get it. Do you want to see me next Tuesday at 11?
C: Don't know.
T: "I just don't know."
   (Silence of 34 seconds has been eliminated from the tape)
T: Right at this point you just don't know... whether you want to say "yes" to that or not, huh? ...I guess you feel so down and so awful that you just don't know whether you can... see that far ahead. Huh?
   (Silence of 1 minute, 5 seconds has been eliminated from the tape)
T: I'm going to give you an appointment at that time because *I'd* sure like to see *you* then.
   (Therapist writing out appointment slip)
   (Silence of 50 seconds has been eliminated from the tape)
T: And another thing I would say is that... if things continue to stay so rough for you, don't hesitate to have them call me. If you should decide to take off, I would very much appreciate if you would have them call me and... so I could see you first. I wouldn't try to dissuade you. I'd just want to see you.
C: I might go today. Where, I don't know, but I don't care.
T: Just feel that your mind is made up and that you're going to... leave. You're not going *to* anywhere. You're just... just going to leave, huh?
   (Silence of 53 seconds has been eliminated from the tape)
C: That's why I want to go, 'cause I don't care what happens.
T: Huh?
C: That's why I want to go, 'cause I don't care what happens.
T: Uh, hum. Uh, hum. That's why you want to go is because you really don't care about yourself. You just don't care what happens. And I guess I'd just like to say... I care about you. And I care what happens.
   (Silence of 30 seconds has been eliminated from the tape)
   (He bursts into tears and unintelligible sobs)
T: Somehow that just... makes all the feelings pour out.
   (Silence of 35 seconds has been eliminated from the tape)
T: And you just weep and weep and weep. And feel so badly.
   (He continues to sob, blows nose, breathes in great gasps)
   (Silence of 34 seconds has been eliminated from the tape)
T: I do get some sense of how awful you feel inside... You just sob and sob.
   (He puts his head on desk close to microphone, which magnifies his gulping, gasping sobs)
   (Silence of 31 seconds has been eliminated from the tape)
T: I guess all the pent-up feelings you've been feeling the last few days just... came rolling out.

(*Blows his nose*)
(*Silence of 32 seconds has been eliminated from the tape*)
T: There's some Kleenex there, if you'd like it… Hum. (sympathetically) You just feel kind of torn to pieces inside.
(*Silence of 1 minute, 56 seconds has been eliminated from the tape*)
C: I wish I could die.
(*Sobbing*)
T: You just wish you could die, don't you? Uh, hum. You just feel so awful, you wish you could perish.
(*Therapist lays his hand gently on Vac's arm during this period. Vac shows no definite response. However, the storm subsides somewhat. Very heavy breathing.*)
(*Silence of 1 minute, 10 seconds has been eliminated from the tape*)
T: You just feel so awful and so torn apart inside that, that it just makes you wish you could pass out.
(*Silence of 3 minutes, 29 seconds has been eliminated from the tape*)
T: I guess life is so tough, isn't it? You just feel you could weep and sob your heart away and wish you could die.
(*Heavy breathing continues*)
(*Silence of 6 minutes, 14 seconds has been eliminated from the tape*)
T: I don't want to rush you, and I'll stay as long as you really need me, but I do have another appointment, that I'm already late for.
C: Yeah.
(*Silence of 17 minutes has been eliminated from the tape*)
T: Certainly been through something, haven't you?
(*Silence of 1 minute, 18 seconds has been eliminated from the tape*)
T: May I see you Tuesday?
C: Yeah.
T: Huh?
C: (unintelligible)
T: I just don't know. Uh, hum. You know all the things I said before, I mean very much. I want to see you Tuesday and I want to see you before then if you want to see me. So, if you need me, don't hesitate to call me.
(*Silence of 1 minute has been eliminated from the tape*)
T: It's really rough, isn't it?
(*Silence of 24 seconds has been eliminated from the tape*)
C: Yes.
T: Sure is.
(*Vac slowly gets up to go*)
(*Silence of 29 seconds has been eliminated from the tape*)
T: Want to take that too?
(*He takes appointment slip*)
(*Silence of 20 seconds has been eliminated from the tape*)
T: There's a washroom right down the hall where you can wash your face.
(*Therapist opens door—noise and voices from corridor*)
(*Silence of 18 seconds has been eliminated from the tape*)
C: You don't have a cigarette, do you?

(Therapist finds one. Noise of microphone being moved.)
T: There's just one. I looked in the package, but... I don't know. I haven't any idea how old it is, but it looks sort of old.
C: I'll see you. (hardly audible)
T: Okay. I'll be looking for you Tuesday, Vac.

Commentary

I was thrilled to read a transcript of therapy sessions with Carl Rogers and a schizophrenic patient. While I work with mostly high-functioning people in my private practice, I have focused on schizophrenia for some part of every week for the past 49 years. Rogers presents two therapy sessions that occur after he and his hospitalized patient had been working together twice a week for 11 months. I will focus this commentary on the striking differences between treatment for schizophrenia in the 1950s and '60s compared with today's treatment and on the enduring wonder of the work.

In today's mental health care system, a person with schizophrenia somehow gets to a hospital (often driven in an ambulance or a police car), is given medicine and spends a few days to two weeks on a hospital ward. That person is then discharged with the name of a psychiatrist for medication management to return to his or her family of origin or supervised living situation. The main ingredient of the work is medicine; new drugs are added on top of old ones because there is no time to take people off their meds and try them on something new. The standard of care for schizophrenia in 2018 is that patients are medicated, quickly discharged from hospitals and not referred for psychotherapy.

In Rogers' account, *not one word is spoken about medicine!* The patient and the doctor say nothing about medicine compliance, side effects, or potential drug changes. In fact, we do not even know if the patient takes medicine. The absence of any mention of drugs or side effects in Rogers' sessions is almost inconceivable for 2018 schizophrenia treatment.

In Rogers' account, the patient has been living in the hospital for two years and a month! That bears repeating: two years and a month! Rogers describes a time where clinicians in a hospital actually got to know their patients; they got to know not only the voices the patients were hearing or the delusions they might fear, but also their families, their interests, their hopes. Furthermore, the patients had the possibility of feeling known; they could slowly grasp that the hospital staff were genuinely trying to understand who they were. In 2018, the focus of psychiatric hospital care is on eliminating the severe symptoms, not on understanding the person. Today, no one stays in a mental hospital for years. In fact, *three months* is considered long. Today, hospital clinicians are talking about discharge before they have barely said hello.

In Rogers' account, the schizophrenic patient is engaged in long-term psychotherapy. Today, people with schizophrenia rarely are in long-term therapy. Insurance companies have concluded that extreme symptoms can be more quickly managed by medicine; therapy is seen as taking too long or as ineffective with this population (as, in fact, Freud believed).

Since Freud's time, we in mental health care have learned that psychotherapy is not a one-size-fits-all endeavor. Rogers excitedly describes a discovery of what might work with hard-to-reach patients: "We have learned to put ourselves, as feeling human beings, into the relationship…" He presents a session where the patient does not say one word for over 35 minutes. Rogers, on the other hand, says many words in that time, asking the patient how he is feeling, proposing possibilities as to what he might be feeling, telling him he cares about him and even wondering out loud if the patient wants him to "shut up." In this session, the patient and the therapist also sit with long periods of silence (13 minutes, 18 minutes). Unlike Freud's blank screen, Rogers brings himself fully into the room. He asks the patient if he wants a cigarette; he offers him magazines. In addition, he shares personal information, saying that he knows "what it's like to feel that you're just *no damn good* to anybody, because there was a time when….I felt that way about *myself*." Rogers extends the allotted session time with the patient. Finally, when the patient is sobbing, Rogers puts his hand on his arm.

This was not traditional psychotherapy then and it is not typical today. Rarely do therapists talk for long periods of time while the patient remains silent; rarely do they share such personal information or go way over the allotted time boundaries; and even more rarely do they touch their patients. Insurance companies and today's society want quick results, not patience. Insurance pays for sessions with strict time boundaries and private practices run more smoothly if those boundaries are kept. Finally, 2018 lawyers and ethicists often challenge any use of touch.

Rogers' presentation of two therapy sessions from the mid-20th century depicts how treatment for schizophrenia has profoundly changed. One could argue that it changed with good intentions. Moving people quickly out of hospitals seemed humane. Finding medicine to calm the severe symptoms seemed compassionate. But some of the change did not benefit people with schizophrenia. People who are delusional or hearing voices or questioning reality need time, honesty, patience and compassion. Certainly, most people do, but higher functioning individuals can learn (in therapy) how to get these from family, from work, from friends. People with schizophrenia often do not have friends or work or good relationships with family. They rely on their clinicians to have time, to describe reality, to be compassionate.

Today, those who work with severely disturbed people do so despite the restrictions from insurance, courtrooms and the medical establishment. Most of us do so because we love the work. I love that my schizophrenic patients are honest with me because their altered reality does not let them be otherwise. They tell me if I look tired or my haircut is bad. I love trying to be honest with them. If my long-term patient asks me if there are recording devices in my office, I do not immediately ask him how come he is wondering about that; instead, I quickly and honestly tell him no and also tell him that he can move every piece of furniture and remove every picture from the walls to see for himself. My constant and long-term honesty can gradually give him an experience of reality, trust and respect.

Rogers' transcripts reminded me of the bond I feel with others who do this work. We certainly do not do it for the money. Given the low economic status of most people with schizophrenia, we are grateful to have other passions to help pay the bills. Rogers' account also helped me remember when I fell in love—and others in the field were in love—with working with seriously troubled people.

—Ann Reifman, PhD

***

Earlier in my career, I did quite a lot of work with people who have schizophrenia, but I'm unfamiliar with the literature published before and during Rogers' research. This makes it hard to evaluate his work within a larger context. That said, my overall impression is of his sincerity and his genuine effort to make person-to-person contact and get to know his patient beyond any diagnosis.

One example:

C: That's why I want to go, 'cause I don't care what happens.

T: I care about you.

After which Mr. Vac bursts into tears. There is a problem though. Rogers works so very hard, perhaps because of his concern, as he writes, to "communicate" his research "to those who are interested in psychotherapy," and perhaps, to make his mark on the field. At times, this seems to make him more audience- than client-centered. In the example above, he makes no attempt to explore what made his patient weep or why. Did he feel understood, or might Rogers' caring have made him feel worse, more unworthy of caring? Instead Rogers reflects back, I must say ad nauseam, and interprets. "You just weep... and feel so badly."

In fact, most of the tape consists of just two interventions... reflecting back and interpreting. He erases long pauses because he's concerned about losing his audience. This seems to prevent him from exercising some curiosity about what Mr. Vac's pauses are for. Even though Rogers' caring comes through, he seems equally intent on trying out his techniques. This makes the occasional genuine contact all the more poignant.

There's a brief, heartfelt connection when he lays his hand on Mr. Vac's arm, and his patient calms down. However, more of the time, for all the silence he allows, he can't seem to prevent himself from a constant barrage of attempts, either by reflecting back or interpreting, to get his patient to talk.

In my experience with people who have schizophrenia, overstimulation of this kind promotes necessary, self-protective withdrawal. It seems to me, however well-meant, Rogers intrudes and controls, thus contradicting his mission to not "impose on the client." Also, though I imagine it was taken for granted at the time, given Rogers' mission to respect and not impose on his client, it's disturbing to find no evidence that Mr. Vac was asked permission to be interviewed, recorded and filmed. I can't imagine that not having some impact on him. It would certainly cause me to shut up.

Many years ago, working as a social worker on a New York City public hospital locked psychiatric ward for schizophrenic patients, it was my job to make contact with my assigned patients and to assess whether they were connected with family, needed referral to some other facility or program, etc. One young man arrived on the unit completely mute. In front of the nursing station was a day room with a large circle of chairs. I knew he knew I was assigned to him because whenever I entered the room and sat down, he quickly stood up and left. A beginning relationship. I started entering the room deliberately choosing a chair as far away as possible from him without looking his way at all. I sat doing paperwork. At first, he would leave after a couple of minutes, but gradually over a period of a week or so, he sat for longer and longer periods of time. Then he allowed me to sit a bit closer, then closer, until after another week or so, we sat about two chairs apart. Parallel play. Several days later, he, not I, began our actual conversation by saying, "I used to read but then I got frostbite."

After he was discharged, he continued to call me about once a month for two years until I left my position at the hospital. We talked about the weather, about life. He complained about the food in whatever facility he was in and let me know when he was sent to a "home" because, living on the streets, he'd gotten frostbite so severe that his feet had to be amputated. He was trying to get used to a wheelchair. He was a sweet, gentle man. Sadly, once I left, since I had no phone number or address for him, we lost contact. I like to think I had as much impact on him as he had on me. More than 30 years later, I remember him still. Perhaps, without realizing it, I benefited from all the research and efforts, including Rogers', that came before me.

—Rhona Engels, MSW, ACSW

* * *

WHAT A LOVELY OPPORTUNITY TO RECONNECT WITH CARL ROGERS, WHO HAD SUCH A PROFOUND IMPACT ON MY EDUCATION AND WORK AS A THERAPIST. I had forgotten how much I, the profession, and for that matter the entire world, owe him. We in the Academy are also in his debt, as he was gracious enough to serve as our first president, lending us gravitas at a formative time.

As I read his introduction to the tape and the transcript of the tape itself, I was struck by his humanity and kindness. They were palpable. Also, I was awed by his courage in working with such a difficult population and doing research on his work at the same time. His willingness to fly in the face of established inquiry into psychotherapy is remarkable and is the reason that scientific or at least empirical investigation of psychotherapy was launched.

I was delighted by his creativity and fearlessness in finding ways to understand what happens in the consulting room. His courage in exposing his work to the public without pretense or subterfuge is a shining example to all of us to let others see what we do, so that we might understand it better and, one would hope, execute it better.

Rogers was prophetic in that his work is experiential, in and of the moment, and mindful long before that approach became the stock in trade of the contemporary approach to psychotherapy.

As a believer in the power of loving clients warts and all (theirs and mine), I was overwhelmed by the intimacy he feels and expresses to his client and how hard he struggles to connect with the client. His work is a beacon.

I found the therapy session heartbreakingly touching. Rogers in all his Rogersness was so brilliantly adept at staying right next to the client despite the client's struggles and wish to escape and flee. Rogers embodies his deep belief in unconditional positive regard, congruence, and accurate empathy. Along with his patience, generosity, and dependability, a therapeutic alliance has clearly emerged with a client who very likely has been rejected and demeaned by more than the friend he talks about.

In this brief excerpt there is so much for all of us to learn about the importance of not being afraid of clients and their problems and issues. We also learn about the necessity to look at our work as dispassionately as possible in order to improve and to be honest with ourselves. Rogers leads us without fear or desire for approbation. His modesty and humility warm me.

One of my favorite memories of him was at my first Academy event, an I&C in New York City in 1980 that Roz Schwartz chaired. There was a dazzling panel, one of whose members was Fritjof Capra. When the panel spoke of their thoughts about what had transpired in their discussion and in being with the Academy, Capra said that the thing that struck him most was that Carl Rogers was sitting in the audience taking notes.

—Murray Scher, PhD

Technology can be our best friend, and technology can also be the biggest party pooper of our lives. It interrupts our own story, interrupts our ability to have a thought or a daydream, to imagine something wonderful, because we're too busy bridging the walk from the cafeteria back to the office on the cell phone.

—Steven Spielberg

Carla R. Bauer

CARLA R. BAUER, LCSW
ATLANTA, GEORGIA
cbauerlcsw@gmail.com

Screen Therapy vs. Face-to-Face: A Case for Nonequivalence

Book Review

Can an optimally effective therapeutic process occur without physical co-presence?

What happens in screen-bound treatment when, as a patient said, there is no potential to 'kiss or kick?'

How is intimacy affected by radically altering the balance between implicit non-verbal communications and the explicit verbal? (Russell, 2015, p. xvii)

Screen Relations: The Limits of Computer-Mediated Psychoanalysis and Psychotherapy
by Gillian Isaacs Russell
Karnac
London
2015, 206 pages

THESE ARE THE KEY QUESTIONS THAT DR. GILLIAN ISAACS RUSSELL EXPLORES IN SCREEN RELATIONS: THE LIMITS OF COMPUTER-MEDIATED PSYCHOANALYSIS AND PSYCHOTHERAPY—questions that she believes have not been adequately examined by those who endorse technology-mediated therapy as equivalent to co-present treatment, questions that must be asked and answered before entering blindly into these modes in lieu of face-to-face therapy.

When I recently received an email offer to upload my professional profile to a service providing pay-by-the minute phone therapy, I cringed. Clearly the sender had not read my profile if she thought this type of teletherapy would be of interest to me. But there are myriad such technology-mediated platforms augmenting, at best, and increasingly replacing face-to-face services, and their number will only grow. Ten days after the teletherapy bid, I had the opportunity to hear Dr. Gillian Isaacs Russell speak to the Atlanta Psychoanalytic Society about her book, *Screen Relations*. Listening, I knew that hers was an important voice on the theme of this *Voices* issue. Too late for soliciting a new article from Dr. Russell, I started reading.

Screen Relations is part of Karnac's Technology and Mental Health series, edited by Jill Savage Scharff, MD, seeking to adapt psychotherapy and psychoanalysis to the technological world of the 21st century. Scharff notes that while the series addresses both the pros and cons of teletherapy, it tends toward a view of equivalence between screen-based and co-present treatment (Series Editors Preface, p. xi). Russell pushes a pause button, inviting the reader/practitioner to more deeply contemplate the limits of technology-mediated treatment, particularly with regard to psychoanalytic or psychodynamic therapy versus more straightforward information-imparting or manualized techniques, how a screen-based process might differ from a co-present one, and what might be lost. Discerning that equivalence has largely been a blind assumption, she delves into the fields of neuroscience, communication studies, infant observation, cognitive science, and human-computer interaction to explore the above questions and more.

Russell is neither Luddite nor anti-technology. Her work arises out of personal experience as a psychoanalyst relocating from London to South Dakota, then Boulder, Colorado, attempting to use technology to continue treatments and supervisions in process. Her book grew out of first-hand experience of computer-mediated psychoanalysis as a different, non-equivalent, process from co-present treatment.

Russell describes her initial research with participants in the China American Psychoanalytic Alliance (CAPA), formed to meet the needs of Chinese mental health professionals for psychoanalytic training and treatment by providing both classes and training analyses via Skype. She recounts frustrations with poor sound, grainy visuals, frequent interruptions and call backs, as well as observations of behavioral departures from traditional co-present practice: forgotten sessions, analysts drinking tea or checking email during session, increased idle chatting to begin sessions, the analyst talking more in general in technology-mediated sessions. Clinical examples quote analysts and patients in technology-mediated treatment describing struggles to guarantee a safe and private environment, a narrowing of focus that impedes reverie, and recognition of the importance of motility as a key feature of presence and experiencing a sense of self. Analysts and patients cite the value of the transitional journey to and from session as part of the therapeutic work. They address the importance of potentiality in the transference, be it the potentiality to kiss or to kick: What does it mean for safety and boundaries if your therapist doesn't touch you because he *can't* or your patient doesn't hug or strike you, not because she tolerates her feelings or differentiates fantasy from reality, but because she *can't* physically touch you? This concept of potentiality references Winnicott's ideas on object-usage and "the developmental necessity of the subject placing the object outside of the area of omnipotent control, to be recognized as an entity in its own right" (p. 40).

Citing Todd Essig, a leading writer on the impacts of technologically-mediated communication, Russell further explores differences between a shared environment and screen-to-screen relating with respect to risk, repleteness, and relational embodiment. She considers the generally accepted elements of therapeutic effectiveness and how these are impacted in technologically-mediated treatment: a safe, facilitating environment; evenly suspended attention and reverie; provision of a new relational experience; interpretation and insight. Citing the paradigm shift within neuroscience from mind-body dualism to embodied cognition, she explores the importance of embodied presence on mirror neurons, implicit and explicit memory systems, implicit processing and right brain communication. She notes how limitations in technology impact a sense of common ground, trust, gaze, and attention, limiting the important functions of mirror neurons and implicit processes in the therapeutic relationship and the experience of intimacy. Drawing parallels between the therapist-patient dyad and the mother-infant dyad, Russell explores layers of presence and the importance of embodiment in the differentiation of self.

In her conclusions, Russell recognizes that technology-mediated treatment can be helpful, particularly when co-present treatment is not available, but deems it a non-equivalent treatment mode, "certainly better than nothing, [but] it should not be offered with the understanding that it is the same thing as co-present treatment" (p. 181). She stresses the importance of recognizing the differences and presenting technology-mediated treatment as an altered, non-equivalent, process to co-present therapy:

> ... the process by which we work using mediation by technology is not the process that occurs between two physically present people in the traditional consulting room. When both analyst and patient are clear about the nature of technological mediation, it makes a space for informed thinking and attention to the impact of the screen on the analytic process (p.159).

Russell's book is a very sound and accessible exploration of both the psychoanalytic- and neuroscience-based reasons why screen relations are not equivalent to co-presence. In her Atlanta presentation, Russell provided some additional examples of research with monkeys demonstrating that fewer mirror neurons fire in video-mediated interactions than when face to face, making a compelling case for non-equivalence. And while much of her focus is on the analytic process, this carries over well to other psychodynamic, relational, and experiential therapies. I encourage those practicing or contemplating computer-mediated therapy to read this book and consider Russell's questions before assuming equivalence. ▼

Intervision

Bob Rosenblatt

What We Have Here Is a Failure To Communicate

BOB ROSENBLATT, PHD: "I have been sitting in my chair delivering individual, couples and group psychotherapy since 1974. Every day is a new adventure. I never know what I am going to learn, teach or feel in any given session. This is what keeps me coming back hour after hour — day after day. Supervision and practice consultation for other mental health practitioners in Washington, DC, and Atlanta, Georgia, make up another part of my professional life. When I am not in my office, I relish time with my family, especially my grandchildren; I enjoy traveling with my wife, golfing with friends and, now, writing about lessons learned over the years in practice."
dr13bob@aol.com

THIS IS A QUOTATION FROM THE 1967 FILM, *Cool Hand Luke*, spoken in the movie first by the jail warden Strother Martin. Later in the film, it is paraphrased by Paul Newman, a stubborn prisoner. I find this a fitting notion when working with a couple. Much of our work with two people is connected in myriad ways to the flaws and empty space in their communication styles. We consistently encounter dyads in which the most important elements of their relationship are not being spoken, either via content or feelings.

The result of this communication gap is typically a corresponding failure of empathy. Hence, the depth of the communication breakdown may be pervasive. Making matters even more complicated is the introduction of another element that inhibits a more intimate and meaningful dialogue. Common examples of these are substance abuse, religious issues, financial difficulties, parents, pornography, and the newest one, technology addiction.

In many instances, these obstacles work for one or both members of the dyad. Each person's approach to decoupling can deal a devastating blow to the other. When we were younger, we developed techniques of defending ourselves from the intrusiveness/engulfment of the other or the potential violence that another can inflict. Frequently, these self-defensive characteristics hold long-lasting significance in our lives. As we age and become more intellectually developed, we commonly maintain these maneuvers. We also cultivate new and improved ways to accomplish our defensive stance in the world. I refer to this process as encapsulation. In our present cultural milieu, one method of encapsulation is technology. The Internet, iPad, cell phone, e-mails, tweets, snapchats, etc., connect us 24 hours a day to the world. This constant contact has the effect of inhibiting our capacity to create intimacy with significant others in our lives in the here and now.

This ongoing struggle with intimate connection stands in the way of the contact needed to develop, grow and sustain healthy, intimate, and substantive relationships with our loved ones. However, our avoidant self is at work too! It keeps us from having to feel exposed, vulnerable, raw and susceptible to being hurt by these significant people. As such, it is extremely difficult to abandon these tried-and-true defensive moves in order to lean into the relationship with vulnerability.

I believe that my role as a couples therapist is to help reduce and/or eliminate these roadblocks to a more meaningful and affirming relationship. This is true whether it be with each participant in the consultation room, or with me as a role model of this deeper interpersonal process. I make every effort to demonstrate engagement by being open, available and fully present. If I am successful at exposing this, then I may have provided a new template for dyadic interaction. My intent is to offer each couple the safety and security to initiate that process with each other. If that occurs, then my role is to officiate and bump each member back on the path of more vulnerability and to engage with greater empathy. If the couple can incorporate these communication tactics, then we really have accomplished something special.

What makes couples therapy complicated is the balance that you have to provide to all three clients: each member of the partnership plus the couple itself. If you can provide balance in this process, then it has the potential to work for all involved.

Read the case that follows. Pay attention to the concepts that I have tried to put forth in this introduction and see if they are present. Read the responses. How might you proceed with this couple? What additional key ingredients would you add to the stew of this case? Would you see them individually and as a couple? What would be your treatment approach? *Share the craft!*

Doris Jackson, PhD

The Case

HOLLY AND ZITA—TWO WHITE WOMEN IN THEIR LATE 40S—CAME TO ME FOR COUPLES THERAPY SEVERAL MONTHS AFTER HOLLY DISCOVERED THAT ZITA HAD BEGUN AN AFFAIR WITH ANOTHER WOMAN. They had been together as a couple for 14 years but always lived separately, each one owning a very nice condo in different areas of the city where I practice. After the discovery of Zita's cheating, they broke up, at Zita's behest. After about six months, during a dinner meeting, Zita—to her surprise—accessed a lot of sad and tender feelings about Holly. She had already ended her affair; she now agreed to start couples therapy.

Both women have successful careers. Zita owns a business which involves her in frequent travel, to the point where she maintains an additional condo in DC. Holly works as an organizational consultant in a branch of the state government here in Boston. Both women are friendly and delightful people, and I enjoy working with them.

Zita often seems to brush away the significance of what she says or does. She has a teasing, flippant manner, to which Holly responds with a ready smile and laughter. However, Holly often wells up with tears during sessions, and at other times struggles with furrowed brow, saying, "I just want to understand what is happening here. I just need an answer." When we began working together she was emphatic about needing to know whether Zita was leaving her or not, whereas Zita was noncommittal and would shrug and say, "Well, we're here," seeming unmoved by Holly's tears. As the work went on Holly showed herself remarkably open to learning new perspectives. She stopped demanding a quick resolution.

The women reported a history of bad fights, which had become more frequent and problematic over several years before the breakup. There was no physical violence, but both agreed the fights left them stymied and hopeless about being understood. When I asked them to reconstruct one of the fights for me, they couldn't do it. The dialog would go something like:

"Remember there was that time we were driving over the bridge and you got so mad at me for checking my phone?"

"No, THAT's not what I was mad about."

"Yes, you were!"

Both agreed that in retrospect the fights were about "stupid stuff."

I had to work to get any acknowledgement of the deeply held pain and resentment that was present in their relationship. Holly felt pain about Zita's affair and their subsequent break-up. She also had longstanding pain about her experience of Zita constantly checking messages and responding to phone calls when they were together.

For her part, Zita resented what she experienced as a long history of being judged and criticized. It was clear that she had a hot-button reaction when she felt Holly was telling her she was not "allowed" to check her phone or respond to business emails. She had a dread of Holly being "disappointed"—which she always translated as a mandate for herself to be different. At one point Zita revealed that, for the two of them ever to live together, she believed she would have to "stop being me" and focus only on Holly. Holly for her part kept saying that was NOT what she wanted, that she just wanted to be able to "talk about it" and negotiate things if she was feeling pushed aside in favor of Zita's phone. But every time she started to voice her feelings, Zita reacted defensively and the conversation turned into a bitter fight.

Holly felt she had been valiantly trying to articulate her needs, with no good outcome. She was genuinely surprised to find out, during our sessions, that Zita had felt so criticized and scolded. Zita felt Holly had "unfair" rules—that it was ok for Holly to check HER emails or respond to HER phone calls, but that if she did so she was condemned. She experienced Holly's expression of feeling as a laying down of rules. Holly insisted that she did understand Zita's need to keep track of calls and respond to business emails, but that she just needed at times to say, "I need your attention." When I asked Zita if she believed that, she said, "Not really."

Several occurrences created some hopeful movement in the therapy. First, Holly expressed genuine remorse that her attempts to "open up conversation" had come across as such negative, nagging criticism. She understood that the way she had expressed her disappointment was creating hurt and anger rather than the communication she wanted-ed. During one very emotional session she made a heartfelt apology. During the weeks of these conversations, Zita reported that Holly's behavior was "sweeter."

Meanwhile, in response to Zita's off-hand comment that she had ADD—something that the two women had often joked about—I loaned her my copy of *Driven to Distraction* (Hallowell and Ratey, 1994), the groundbreaking book about adult ADD. Both women devoured it in the first week, returned my copy and bought their own. Zita completed the "test" in the book and began to seriously consider that the diagnosis fit her. This perspective allowed us to understand Zita's distractible behavior as something integral to her way of being in the world, rather than as something personal to Holly and the relationship. She said, "I just CAN'T sit still during a long car ride." She seemed to feel less shame, more of a right to feel that way. I believe she has become expert at deflecting criticism with a joke or with a change of subject—strategies that can only take you so far in an intimate relationship.

The authors of the book make a strong point of the lifelong burden for those with ADD being corrected and told they were not paying enough attention, not behaving properly. We speculated that this history might explain how quickly and painfully defensive Zita could become when asked to adjust her behavior. It also allowed Holly to take less personally Zita's distractibility and her inability to sit still and focus on one thing. Both women expressed an enlarged sense of understanding. In a recent session they reported a "very emotional" conversation in which they successfully expressed their differences and reached a resolution—something that felt new.

I have encouraged Zita to seek a consult from an ADD expert, and she is interested in the possibility of a support group. There remains much work for the couples treatment, including taking a true account of the impact of the affair. I am hopeful that their newfound positive experiences of conflict resolution may make this possible. In particular, the two seem to have reached a compromise solution for the checking of emails.

References
Hallowell, E.M., & Ratey, J.J. (1994). *Driven to distraction: Recognizing and coping with attention deficit disorder from childhood through adulthood.* New York: Pantheon Books.

* * *

Response 1

AFTER RE-READING THIS CASE SEVERAL TIMES, I STILL HAD DIFFICULTY BEING INSPIRED TO COMMENT. Then I pondered my own resistance in light of the issues the couple presented. They are not unlike many couples I've treated, whether they are lesbian, gay, straight or anywhere in between. Couples often present with a problem they want solved quickly to make the pain end. It's almost never clear at the beginning whether they are interested in doing the kind of therapy necessary to address the strong primitive forces awakened by a primary relationship.

Zita's possible diagnosis of ADD or ADHD is impacting the couple powerfully and deserves exploration, diagnosis, and possible treatment with medication and behavioral interventions. I was glad to hear their excitement about this possibility and how it would help their understanding of each other and how they function as a couple. Being either ADD or a partner of a person with ADD is a challenging experience for anyone and will be so for this couple. The thrill of getting a clearer picture and a name (ADD) for what seems to be going on is unlikely to last. Before we talk about the deeper work involved, let me address the cell phone issue straight on.

Cell phone habits are a special challenge for a person with ADD. Mobile phones are a major, and relatively new, chunk of most of our lives and many of us are more or less addicted to the immediate gratification this communication vehicle offers. When one is highly distractible, the difficulty quickly multiplies. But as difficult and impactful as this problem is for them, they have already made useful steps in communicating differently about it and easing up on the blame and guilt they previously endured. I see this as a positive sign too.

I don't know what this couple wants other than to stop the punishing fights and have an amiable, albeit distant, connection. It's amazing to me that this has worked for 14 years! At this point in the treatment, I would reinforce their learning more about ADD and its effect on each of them, separately and together. And I would let them know that they are at a decision point in the therapy.

I would offer the idea that, while the fights about cell phone usage are partly about ADD and partly about the addictive/demanding nature of cell phones in general, those arguments are not about "stupid stuff" at all. They are likely a screen for much deeper issues. In my opinion the couple is using the cellphone conflict as a familiar script, both to approach, and simultaneously avoid, addressing the deeper issues at hand—engulfment and abandonment. Zita seems terrified to let Holly express her feelings of disappointment, let alone abandonment, resents the responsibility she feels for accommodating Holly, and moves even further away. For example, when Holly expressed her heartfelt apology, Zita experienced her as being "sweeter." They are repeatedly replicating the exquisitely painful circle that has one member of the unit, perhaps unknowingly, stimulate the other's terror. Then that member reacts out of her terror and that reaction stimulates her partner's terror.

In the past they appear to have mollified each other enough to establish a somewhat satisfying relationship. But I see Zita's affair as a signal that prior modifications are no longer working for them and haven't for a while. Until they understand on a deep emotional level each of their parts of a dynamic they continue to act out with each other, they will not achieve the trust and intimacy they may desire. It is this deep work that will be necessary to understand and grieve the affair. In this formulation Holly is as responsible as Zita for the underlying dynamic that laid the groundwork for Zita's affair, an all too common alarm bell that signals intolerable discomfort in the relationship.

Even though I have written this formulation as though it were reality, it is merely my opinion out of many that are possible. My own former resistance to writing a comment is now clearer to me. I have no passion for working on behavioral problems. In fact, I get bored and restless and begin to distance myself. The therapy usually ends soon unless I am willing to shake things up and challenge the status quo. That option seems to have worked for my resistance here as well.

—Lorraine Hallman, PhD

Response 2

I FIND THIS CASE INTERESTING AND SOMEWHAT CHALLENGING. Perhaps the therapist, because of her need for brevity, left important facts and process out. It seems she was able to have a good working alliance with Holly and Zita. Within the therapy there was effective and positive movement reported by the clients.

It appears that issues around intimacy need to be further addressed.

We have a couple who have been in a long-term relationship yet continue to live apart without any resolution. This is also true of their interactions, e.g., Zita's relationship with her phone.

I am curious how or if the therapist explored their attractions to each other and especially the dynamics of Zita's affair. I consistently felt the therapist stayed away from deeper psychodynamics in favor of a more practical stance. How far a therapist should or needs to go in exploration of any issue is a familiar dilemma. This could be seen in the "fight." The therapist got them to acknowledge the "pain" but stayed with their relationship without exploring either's personal history and meanings. I believe further exploration can be helpful in creating an environment and opportunity for relationship deepening.

With regard to Zita's ADD, paying attention to this physical issue did appear to have very positive results, especially with the use of the book. It does point to the issue of how a therapist deals with the issues of the physical vis-a-vis the psychological. I believe these issues require a kind of differential diagnosis: "You have ADD, but let's look at how you both live with it, how you interpret it and then what you could do."

The therapist perspective on sexuality was not mentioned. I am curious how it affected the treatment. I would like to know more of the therapist's attitudes and feelings. This is one of the issues I would deal with if I were supervising. In supervision it would be helpful to explore with the therapist her attitudes, feelings, and expectations of the clients. What were the counter-transference issues, especially depending on the therapist's own sexual orientation?

In my work and life, I have focused on inner tensions. Dreams, stirred complexes, and affect are useful tools. For me therapy is so much more than a report! I love to hear and experience the internal challenges patients experience in their journeys, which I felt the therapist could have either done or written about more.

—Arthur S. Weinfeld, EdD

Response 3

A LONG TIME AGO IN A GALAXY FAR, FAR AWAY, I WAS A YOUNG AND NOVICE THERAPIST. This was especially true when it came to offering couples therapy. One of my first enduring lessons arose when I attended an AAP Institute and Conference in Toronto. I was siting next to Dr. Mildred Kagan, an Atlanta-based couples therapist. She was probably in her 70s at this time and was a seasoned veteran of our craft. Neither of us believed the co-presenters in the couples therapy demonstration were powerful or effective. At some point, Millie turned to me and said, "Couples therapy is easy!"

I was surprised but definitely interested in her viewpoint and said, "Do tell!"

Dr. Kagan explained, "All you have to do is elicit the three F's to be successful in treating couples."

And then she shared the three F's. They were Fun, Fighting and Fucking. She believed that if these three elements are present, the couple will have the capacity to survive many common relational pitfalls. The creation of a substantive relationship as well as the capacity to sustain emotional intimacy will be enabled by these simple three F's.

Couples work is inherently complicated. There are three clients in the room. Each side of the couple and the couple make three. By the time most couples arrive at one's door, the ruts that have been developed in their relationship are well-worn and automatic. Helping the couple to backfill these ruts is hard work for all parties. This process involves a deep understanding of each person's basic character structure that has shaped the way they relate to each other. It also includes helping the partners experiment with new and more effective ways of being in relation.

So, how does my little story of the three F's apply to the case of Holly and Zita? It was not evident in the case write-up that Holly and Zita were having much fun. It was clear that they did not fight fairly or effectively. In addition, the case presenter does not give any information on the third "F." I wondered about their sexual relationship since they lived separately and one member of the couple had acted out. There had to be something missing in the emotional and physical elements of their relationship that was the basis of this physical disconnection. Is it due to unexpressed anger? Is it due to an inability to be present and emotionally expressive with each other? Is it due to one member of the couple being deeply dissatisfied with their appetite for engagement? Do they feel unappreciated by the other, which usually washes over into resentment? Is one of them scared of intimacy and engulfment? These are a sampling of the questions that would have to be directly addressed in couples therapy.

There are numerous indicators of the schism in Holly and Zita's connection. Here are the first three from the case presentation. The intervention using bibliotherapy with respect to the ADD is spot-on and definitely a necessary treatment path. I am sure it was helpful in addressing this matter and helped diminish the split. However, this track might allow Zita to use her ADD as a significant excuse for a lack of capacity to be interpersonal. Second, cellphones— as is all technology—are powerful distractions that may also serve to avoid contact. Human beings are far more efficient in developing obstacles to intimacy then being open to deep connection.

Third, separate living arrangements for the duration of their relationship is another strong indicator of a powerful disconnection. All of these elements illuminate the divide and require attention by all parties during the treatment process. Thematically, what needs to be the focus of the couple's work? Holly and Zita's fear of intimacy is pervasive and has to be a primary objective of the therapy.

The therapist clearly likes Holly and Zita but appears hesitant to confront them with the notion that both have significantly contributed to the rift in their relationship. As is true for many couples, each half usually wants to place the lion's share of blame on her partner. It is a rare occurrence when, at the beginning of therapy, either member of the couple is willing to examine their contribution and responsibility for the problems. All parties are more typically concerned with being wrong and/or blamed. This defensive path is a consistently untenable road for any couple. It must be modified.

Moving this couple forward is accomplished by addressing the dynamic of intimacy versus isolation. Each member of any couple needs to independently express their aversion to the other as well their deep hunger for the other. As these personal feelings emerge, each partner has the opportunity to respond with empathy to the emotional elements of the other's story. One important aspect of couples therapy is to offer each individual the possibility to bear witness to the pain/angst of the other. Most couples arrive at our door with a deep failure in empathy. Bringing empathy to the couple's interaction is a deeply healing part of the therapy.

In the case presentation, it was unclear if the therapist had gotten to these themes in her work with Holly and Zita. The treatment elements highlighted in my response are common mileposts encountered during any treatment process with couples. The therapist is dealing with two strong and intelligent women who are unsure and unskilled at fostering the deeper connection. The couples therapist had her work cut out with this pair. The therapist needs to slow Holly and Zita down in order to backfill the enormous gaps in their relationship. Holly and Zita need individualized attention regarding their separate character struggles with intimacy. With this as one component in the treatment plan, then the complicated process of couples work could proceed as well.

—Robert Rosenblatt, PhD

WTF?!? Oppression, Freedom, and Self
Voices, Winter 2018

Call for Papers

IN THE AGE OF TRUMPOCRACY, WHITE NATIONALISM, #MeToo, pussy hats, anti-immigration, xenophobia, the wall, fake news, diversity training, sexual harassment training, LGBTQ awareness—many of us are spinning. A sometimes-nauseating whirl of every-flavored politics, social turmoil, and a never-still news cycle permeates our day.

What's going on? Has our world changed, or is an ignored raw edge becoming more visible? What changes seem growthful or healing, which damage and diminish? What does this look like in our offices, with clients swimming in the same soup as us? How does working in an altered environment affect you and your patients? As a healing community, is it ethical to maintain our supposed neutrality? Can we help the individual—or the larger society—make sense of this experience?

Even as what seems a bullying atmosphere tears at the societal and relational fabric of our lives and work, perhaps there is a process at hand. In therapy, we know that difficult work brings insight, relief, and change; it's a process in which we discover our self-imposed oppression and seek more freedom to be our true selves. Is it possible that our current mess is a bigger version of a similar process? At the public level, can we engage with the "other" in a way that leads us to something better?

We seek a true self (or a manageable national identity) as we grapple with oppression and strive for freedom—*whatever* your perspective is—at the local, national and global level or in our and our clients' personal work. For this issue of *Voices*, consider what that means in your life and practice.

Voices welcomes submissions in the form of personal essay, research- and case-based inquiry, poetry, art, cartoons and photography.

Deadline for submission:
August 15, 2018
Direct questions and submissions to the editor, Kristin Staroba
kristin.staroba@gmail.com

See Submission Guidelines on the AAP website:
www.aapweb.com.

Subscribe to Voices

The American Academy of Psychotherapists invites you to be a part of an enlightening journey into...

VOICES

Voices is a uniquely rewarding publication providing a meeting ground with other experienced psychotherapists. A theme-oriented journal, *Voices* presents personal and experiential essays by therapists from a wide range of orientations. Each issue takes you on an intimate journey through the reflections of therapists as they share their day-to-day experiences in the process of therapy. *Voices'* contributors reveal insights inherent in our lives, our culture and our society.

As a subscriber, you'll have the opportunity to experience contributions from noted luminaries in psychotherapy. Using various styles from articles to poems, *Voices* is interdisciplinary in its focus, reflecting the aims and mission of its publisher, the American Academy of Psychotherapists.

VOICES **SUBSCRIPTION**

Please start my one-year subscription to AAP's journal *Voices* at $65 for individuals PDF only; $85 for individuals PDF & print copy. Institutional subscriptions may be reserved directly through the AAP office or through the traditional subscription agencies at $249 per year. *Voices* is published electronically three times per year and is delivered to your email address as an ePublication.

Name
Address
City   State   ZIP
Telephone   Fax
Email

❏ My check made payable to AAP *Voices* is enclosed.
❏ Please charge to my credit card, using the information I have supplied below:
Form of payment: ❏ Master Card   ❏ Visa
Account #   Expiration:
Signature

Address all orders by mail to:
Voices
230 Washington Ave Ext, Suite 101
Albany, NY 12203
You may also fax your order to (518) 240-1178.
For further information, please call (518) 694-5360

Guidelines for Contributors

Voices: The Art and Science of Psychotherapy, is the journal of the American Academy of Psychotherapists. Written by and for psychotherapists and healing professionals, it focuses on therapists' personal struggles and growth and on the promotion of excellence in the practice of psychotherapy. The articles are written in a personalized voice rather than an academic tone, and they are of an experiential and theoretical nature that reflects on the human condition.

Each issue has a central theme as described in the call for papers. Manuscripts that fit this theme are given priority. Final decision about acceptance must wait until all articles for a particular issue have been reviewed. Articles that do not fit into any particular theme are reviewed and held for inclusion in future issues on a space available basis.

Articles. See a recent issue of *Voices* for general style. Manuscripts should be double-spaced in 12 point type and no longer than 4,000 words (about 16 to 18 pages). Do not include the author's name in the manuscript, as all submissions receive masked review by two or more members of the Editorial Review Board. Keep references to a minimum and follow the style of the *Publication Manual of the American Psychological Association, 5th ed.*

Submit via email, attaching the manuscript as a Word document file. Send it to Kristin Staroba *(kristin.staroba@gmail.com)*. Put "Voices" in the email's subject line, and in the message include the author's name, title and degree, postal address, daytime phone number, manuscript title, and word count. Please indicate for which issue of *Voices* the manuscript is intended.

If a manuscript is accepted, the author will be asked to provide a short autobiographical sketch (75 words or less) and a photograph that complies with technical quality standards outlined in a PDF which will be sent to you.

Neither the editorial staff nor the American Academy of Psychotherapists accepts responsibility for statements made in its publication by contributors. We expect authors to make certain there is no breach of confidentiality in their submissions. Authors are responsible for checking the accuracy of their quotes, citations, and references.

Poetry. We welcome poetry of high quality relevant to the theme of a particular issue or the general field of psychotherapy. Short poems are published most often.

Book and Film Reviews. Reviews should be about 500 to 750 words, twice that if you wish to expand the material into a mini-article.

Visual Arts. We welcome submissions of photographs or art related to the central theme for consideration. Electronic submissions in JPEG or TIFF format are required. If you would like to submit images, please request the PDF of quality standards from Mary de Wit at *md@in2wit.com* or find it on *www.aapweb.com*. Images are non-returnable and the copyright MUST belong to the submitting artist.

Copyright. By submitting materials to *Voices* (articles, poems, photos or artwork), the author transfers and consents that copyright for that article will be owned by the American Academy of Psychotherapists, Inc.

American Academy of Psychotherapists

Vision Statement
Our vision is to be the premier professional organization where therapeutic excellence and the use of self in psychotherapy flourish.

Mission Statement
The mission of the American Academy of Psychotherapists is to invigorate the psychotherapist's quest for growth and excellence through authentic interpersonal engagement.

Core Values
- Courage to risk and willingness to change
- Balancing confrontation and compassion
- Commitment to authenticity with responsibility
- Honoring the individual and the community

Full Membership
Full Membership in the Academy requires a doctoral or professional degree in one of the following mental health fields: psychiatry, clinical or counseling psychology, social work, pastoral counseling, marriage and family therapy, counseling, or nursing, and licensure which allows for the independent practice of psychotherapy.
- Specific training in psychotherapy with a minimum of 100 hours of supervision.
- At least one year of full-time post graduate clinical experience (or the equivalent in part-time experience) for doctoral level applicants, at least two years for others.
- A minimum of 100 hours of personal psychotherapy.

A person who does not fulfill the above requirements but who is able to document a reasonable claim for eligibility, such as a distinguished contributor to the field of psychotherapy, may also be considered for full membership.

Other Categories of Membership
In the interest of promoting the development of experienced psychotherapists, one category of associate membership is offered for those with the intent of becoming full members. These members will be working with a mentor as they progress to Full Membership.

Associate Membership
- has completed a relevant professional degree
- is currently practicing psychotherapy under supervision appropriate to the licensure
- has recommendations from at least three faculty, supervisors, and/or Academy members
- has completed or is actively engaged in obtaining 100 hours of personal psychotherapy
- agrees to work with an Academy member mentor
- may be an associate for no more than five years

Student Affiliate
For students currently enrolled in a graduate degree program. Application includes acceptable recommendations from two faculty, supervisors or Academy members.

For information regarding membership requirements or to request an application, contact the Central Office. Membership information and a printable application form are also available on the Academy's Web site, www.aapweb.com.

Executive Offices
aap@caphill.com
230 Washington Ave Ext, Suite 101
Albany, NY 12203
Phone (518) 240-1178
Fax (518) 463-8656

2018 Officers
Doug Cohen, PhD
President

Gordon Cohen, PsyD
Immediate Past President

David Donlon, LCSW
President-Elect

Diane Shaffer, PsyD
Secretary

Steven Ingram, D Min
Treasurer

Executive Council
2017 – 2020
David Pellegrini, PhD
Lori Oshrain, PhD
Tandy Levine, LCSW

2015 – 2018
Ellen Carr, MSW
Jacob Megdell, PhD

2016 – 2018
Judy Lazarus, MSW

2016 – 2019
Neil Makstein, PhD
Stephanie Spalding, LCSW
Linda Tillman, PhD

Made in the USA
Columbia, SC
17 June 2018